JOURNEY TO THE MANGER: A 25-DAY FAMILY ADVENTURE

By Angelina D'Alessandro

Journey to the Manger: A 25-Day Family Adventure
© 2025 Angelina D'Alessandro
All rights reserved.

No part of this publication may be reproduced, stored in a retrieval system, or transmitted in any form or by any means, electronic, mechanical, photocopying, recording, or otherwise, without prior written permission from the publisher, except in the case of brief quotations used in critical articles or reviews.

Scripture Notice

Core scripture readings and quoted passages from the books of Luke and Matthew, along with supporting verses from Isaiah, Micah, John, Psalms, and 2 Corinthians, are quoted from the *New International Version (NIV®)*.

Scripture quotations taken from *The Holy Bible, New International Version®, NIV®*. Copyright © 1973, 1978, 1984, 2011 by Biblica, Inc. Used with permission of Zondervan. All rights reserved worldwide. www.zondervan.com

Cover design & interior layout by Angelina D'Alessandro
Published by D'Alessandro Publishing
ISBN: 979-8-9988796-1-6
Printed in the United States of America

AI Tools Disclosure
Some visual and creative content in this publication was developed in collaboration with AI-assisted tools, including Canva and ChatGPT. All final text, design, and editorial decisions were made by Angelina D'Alessandro, who assumes full responsibility for the completed work.

TABLE OF CONTENTS

Day 1: **The Promise of a Savior** *Isaiah 9:2-7*

Day 2: **A Messenger from Heaven** *Luke 1:26-38*

Day 3: **Mary's Song of Joy** *Luke 1:46-55*

Day 4: **Joseph's Dream** *Matthew 1:18-25*

Day 5: **The Journey Begins** *Luke 2:1-5*

Day 6: **The Star of Bethlehem** *Matthew 2:1-2*

Day 7: **No Room at the Inn** *Luke 2:6-7*

Day 8: **Shepherds in the Night** *Luke 2:8-12*

Day 9: **A Heavenly Choir** *Luke 2:13-14*

Day 10: **The Christmas Tree** *Psalm 1:3; John 3:16*

Day 11: **The Good News Spreads** *Luke 2:15-18*

Day 12: **Mary Treasures It All** *Luke 2:19-20*

Day 13: **God's Perfect Timing** *Galatians 4:4-5*

Day 14: **The Candy Cane** *John 10:11*

Day 15: **Gifts Fit for a King** *Matthew 2:9-11*

Day 16: **A Warning in the Night** *Matthew 2:12-13*

Day 17: **The Family Flees to Egypt** *Matthew 2:14-15*

Day 18: **The Wreath** *Isaiah 9:6*

Day 19: **Return to Nazareth** *Matthew 2:19-23*

Day 20: **Simeon and Anna Rejoice** *Luke 2:25-38*

Day 21: **The Name Above All Names** *Philippians 2:9-11*

Day 22: **The Poinsettia** *2 Corinthians 9:15*

Day 23: **The Greatest Gift of All** *John 3:16*

Day 24: **The Manger Moment** *Luke 2:6-7*

Day 25: **The Morning of Christmas** *Luke 2:8-20*

Bonus Pages
- "Before You Begin" Family Guide
- Advent Tracker Page
- Family Coloring & Doodle Pages
- "Advent Extras"— located at the back of this devotional

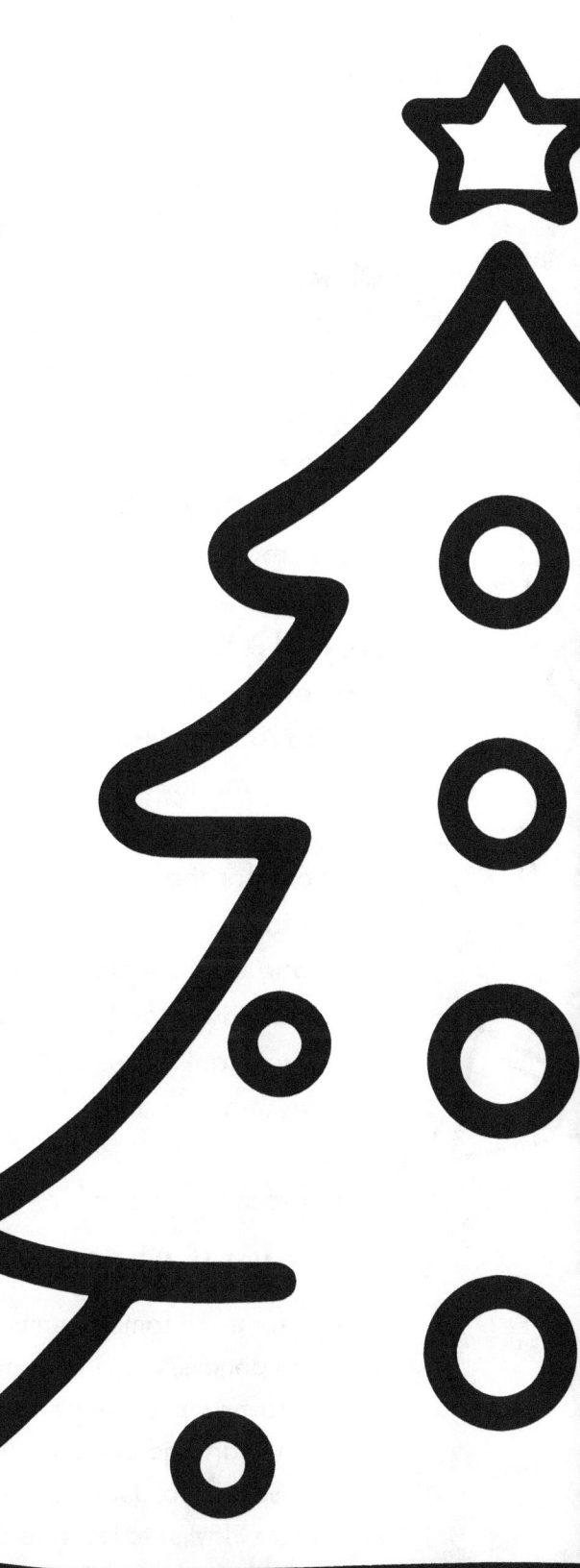

BEFORE YOU BEGIN: A FAMILY GUIDE

Christmas isn't just about twinkling lights, presents, and songs we love; it's about the miracle of Jesus coming close to us. This 25-day journey is your family's invitation to slow down, gather close, and walk together toward the manger.

Each day will bring a short Scripture reading, a reflection or journaling moment, and a fun interactive activity. You'll learn, laugh, pray, and, most of all, draw nearer to Jesus together.

HOW TO USE THIS BOOK

1. **Choose a Time Together**: Pick a cozy moment each day, before school, after dinner, or before bedtime. Keep it consistent so it becomes a family rhythm.
2. **Begin with the Countdown**: Start with the day's coloring page. Read it aloud and talk about what it means. Color in each day on your Advent Tracker Page to mark your progress.
3. **Read the Story**: Open your Bibles to the listed passage (*Luke* or *Matthew*). Read the verses together, then use the Family Read-Aloud Summary to briefly revisit what you read and reflect on the heart of the story as a family.
4. **Journal & Reflect**: Take a few quiet moments for each person to write or draw in their own Bible or notebook. You'll find journaling prompts designed for all ages.
5. **Do the Activity**: Every day includes something interactive, crafts, games, acts of kindness, music, or storytelling moments. These help connect the Bible story to everyday life.
    - Look for the ☆ symbol! On certain days, you'll find a special Tradition Day. These entries explore the meaning behind beloved Christmas traditions, like the candy cane, the Christmas tree, and the star itself. Each one includes a short devotion, fun activity, and a family connection moment to help you see how these symbols point back to Jesus. You can spot these days marked with a ☆ throughout the devotional pages.
6. **Pray Together**: Close your time by saying the day's prayer or blessing. You might even create your own!

WHAT YOU'LL NEED

- A Bible for each family member (or one to share)
- Coloring pencils, crayons, or markers
- A few craft supplies (paper, glue, scissors, nothing fancy!)
- An open heart and a few minutes together each day.
- Search Spotify for Journey to the Manger: A 24-Day Family Adventure Playlist to listen to the daily songs as you go. Each track is listed in your Advent Tracker for easy reference.

December 1 – 12

Act of Kindness: Say "thank you" to someone who helps you.
Song of the Day: "O Come, O Come, Emmanuel"

Act of Kindness: Do one thing today that makes someone feel loved.
Song of the Day: "Mary, Did You Know?"

Act of Kindness: Make someone smile by telling a joke, giving a compliment, or sharing joy.
Song of the Day: "Joy to the World"

Act of Kindness: Help with a task without being asked. Quietly serve someone.
Song of the Day: "O Little Town of Bethlehem"

Act of Kindness: Pray for someone who might be far from home or lonely.
Song of the Day: "Away in a Manger"

Act of Kindness: Be a light today, do something kind when no one's watching.
Song of the Day: "Christmas Canon"

Act of Kindness: Make space for someone, invite someone to join a game or talk.
Song of the Day: "Silent Night"

Act of Kindness: Share hope today, remind someone that good things can still happen.
Song of the Day: "Go Tell It on the Mountain"

Act of Kindness: Leave a kind note or message for someone to find.
Song of the Day: "Angels We Have Heard on High"

Act of Kindness: Be generous today, with your words, patience, or time.
Song of the Day: "O Tannenbaum"

Act of Kindness: Tell someone, "I'm thankful for you."
Song of the Day: "We Wish You a Merry Christmas"

Act of Kindness: Take a moment to thank someone who blesses your life
Song of the Day: "What Child Is This?"

The best part of the story is still ahead...

December 13 – 25

Act of Kindness: Share something special with someone.
Song of the Day: "Come Thou Long Expected Jesus"

Act of Kindness: Give a candy cane (or treat) to someone.
Song of the Day: "The First Noel"

Act of Kindness: Serve someone for Jesus today.
Song of the Day: "O Come, All Ye Faithful"

Act of Kindness: Pray for someone who needs protection.
Song of the Day: "It Came Upon the Midnight Clear"

Act of Kindness: Be gentle with someone who seems upset or afraid today.
Song of the Day: "God Rest Ye Merry, Gentlemen"

Act of Kindness: Bring peace to someone today, share, help, or mend a hurt.
Song of the Day: "Hark! The Herald Angels Sing"

Act of Kindness: Do something that makes home feel more loving, help cook, tidy, or make a cozy space.
Song of the Day: "I'll Be Home for Christmas"

Act of Kindness: Do something thoughtful for an older neighbor or family member, call, visit, or write a note.
Song of the Day: "Angels from the Realms of Glory"

Act of Kindness: Tell someone what you appreciate about them today.
Song of the Day: "Carol of the Bells"

Act of Kindness: Give a handmade or heartfelt gift; draw a picture, write a card, or bake a treat.
Song of the Day: "Do You Hear What I Hear?"

Act of Kindness: Do one act of kindness for someone without telling them.
Song of the Day: "The Little Drummer Boy"

Act of Kindness: Give five minutes to pray or help someone prepare for Christmas morning.
Song of the Day: "O Holy Night"

DAY 1   THE PROMISE OF A SAVIOR   ISAIAH 9:2-7

"The people walking in darkness have seen a great light; on those living in the land of deep darkness a light has dawned." — Isaiah 9:2 (NIV)

BEFORE YOU BEGIN

Find your Advent Tracker and color in Day 1 to celebrate the start of your journey together. Then read the verse at the top of the page, your Guiding Verse for today, and imagine how it must have felt to wait for a promise like that, a promise of hope, peace, and light.

THE READING - A PROMISE OF LIGHT

Long before the first Christmas, the world felt heavy and dark. God's people were waiting for someone who could save them, guide them, and bring peace again. Then one day, through a prophet named Isaiah, God spoke a promise that changed everything: a Savior was coming!

Through Isaiah, God reminded His people that He had not forgotten them. The light was on its way, a light so bright it would reach into every heart, every home, and every generation to come.

Read Isaiah 9:2-7 together. As you read, imagine what it would feel like to be waiting for hope to arrive, and then to hear this beautiful promise for the first time.

FAMILY READ-ALOUD SUMMARY

God's people were waiting for help. The world felt dark and broken, but Isaiah gave them hope; a Savior was coming! Jesus would be born to bring peace, joy, and light to everyone who believes in Him.

STUDY & REFLECTION ON ISAIAH 9:2-7

All suggestions are optional; the most important thing is interacting with God's Word and connecting with what He wants to show you today.

KEY THEMES

- God's promises are trustworthy.
- Jesus is the Light that breaks through darkness.
- Hope often begins before we see the answer.

1. **Read the passage slowly** — Isaiah 9:2-7. Pause at any verse or word that catches your attention. (Example: "The people walking in darkness have seen a great light.")

2. **Write or draw the verse or phrase in your Bible margin or journal.** Under it, write a short thought or prayer about why it matters to you. (Example: "God, help me see Your light even when I feel unsure.")

3. **Make the connection** - Ask yourself: "Where do I need God's light in my life right now?" Write, draw, or talk about your answer together.

PRACTICAL APPLICATION

Think about something you've been waiting for, maybe an answer, healing, or a change. Ask yourself: Can I trust God's timing here?

- Today, when you start to feel impatient, whisper:

"GOD IS WORKING, EVEN WHEN I CAN'T SEE IT."

TEACHING POINTS

1. Isaiah's prophecy reminds us that even when God seems silent, His plan is still unfolding. The people of Israel waited hundreds of years, yet God's promise never failed.
2. Advent teaches us to wait with hope, not in fear, but in faith that God always keeps His word.

SCRIPTURE CONNECTION

"In Him was life, and that life was the light of all mankind. The light shines in the darkness, and the darkness has not overcome it." John 1:4-5 (NIV)

FAMILY STUDY QUESTIONS

(Choose one or two to discuss together.)

1. What do you think it felt like for people to wait for God's promise?
2. Why do you think light is such a good picture of Jesus?
3. How can our family be a light to someone this week?

FAMILY FAITH IN ACTION

Option 1: Follow the Light (Action Game)
Supplies: Flashlight or LED candle.

1. Choose one person to hide the light somewhere in the room.
2. Everyone else searches silently to find it.
3. When someone finds it, they say one word that describes Jesus (hope, peace, love, joy).
4. Repeat so each person gets a turn to hide the light.

Connection:
Just as God's people searched for hope in dark times, we can always look for His light and truth, even when it's hidden.

Option 2: Promise Ornament (Craft)
Supplies: Paper circles, ribbon or string, markers, and scissors.

1. Cut out a circle and write "God keeps His promises" in the center.
2. Around it, draw or write ways you've seen God keep His promises, big or small.
3. Punch a hole at the top, thread a ribbon, and hang your ornament where you'll see it every day.

Connection:
Every time you see your Promise Ornament, remember that God's light and love never fade, His promises always shine true.

PERSONAL REFLECTION

Before you pray, take a moment to write or draw:
- What stood out to you most today?

- What prayer request or need is on your heart tonight?

(Encourage each family member to write or share aloud if they'd like.)

FAMILY PRAYER TIME

Choose one person to lead the prayer tonight.
It can be as simple as thanking God for His promises or asking Him to help you shine His light this week.

DAY 2   A MESSENGER FROM HEAVEN   LUKE 1:26-38

"Greetings, you who are highly favored! The Lord is with you." — Luke 1:28 (NIV)

BEFORE YOU BEGIN

Color in Day 2 on your Advent Tracker to mark your progress. Then read today's verse aloud and take a quiet moment to imagine how Mary must have felt hearing those words, surprised, unsure, yet chosen by God.

THE READING - A MESSAGE THAT CHANGED EVERYTHING

God chose an ordinary young woman for an extraordinary purpose. When the angel Gabriel appeared to Mary, he brought good news that would change the world forever; she would give birth to Jesus, the Son of God.

At first, Mary was afraid. But Gabriel reminded her, "The Lord is with you." And with that promise, courage began to grow in her heart. Mary didn't understand everything, but she said yes to God anyway.

Read Luke 1:26-38 together. As you read, notice how many times the angel reminds Mary that God's plan is full of peace, not fear.

FAMILY READ-ALOUD SUMMARY

An angel named Gabriel brought Mary a message from God; she would be the mother of Jesus! Even though it was surprising and a little scary, Mary trusted God and said yes to His plan.

STUDY & REFLECTION ON LUKE 1:26-38

All suggestions are optional; the most important thing is interacting with God's Word and connecting with what He wants to show you today.

1. **Read the passage slowly** — Luke 1:26-38. Pause when you hear something that makes you wonder or feel amazed. (Example: "Do not be afraid, Mary; you have found favor with God.")

2. **Write or draw the verse or phrase in your Bible margin or journal.** Under it, write (or say aloud) one way you can show trust in God this week, even if you don't understand everything.

3. **Make the connection** - Ask yourself: "When have I felt afraid to say yes to something God wanted me to do?" Write, draw, or talk about your answer together.

TEACHING POINTS

1. When the angel appeared to Mary, his message changed everything. God chose an ordinary young woman for an extraordinary purpose, reminding us that He can use anyone who trusts Him.
2. Gabriel told Mary, "Do not be afraid." God knew she would need courage to say yes. Like Mary, we can believe that when God calls us, He will give us what we need to follow Him, even when we don't see the whole picture.

FAMILY STUDY QUESTIONS

(Choose one or two to discuss together.)

1. Why do you think Mary was afraid at first?
2. What does it mean to trust God even when we don't know what's ahead?
3. How can we be "messengers of good news" in our home or school this week?

KEY THEMES

- God calls ordinary people for extraordinary purposes.
- Saying "yes" to God takes courage and faith.
- God's messages always bring peace, not fear.

PRACTICAL APPLICATION

Mary's story shows us that trusting God doesn't mean we stop feeling afraid; it means we choose faith in the middle of fear.

- When something feels uncertain this week (a big decision, a change, a challenge at school or work), take one deep breath and whisper:

"THE LORD IS WITH ME."

SCRIPTURE CONNECTION

"Do not be anxious about anything, but in every situation, by prayer and petition, with thanksgiving, present your requests to God.
And the peace of God, which transcends all understanding, will guard your hearts and your minds in Christ Jesus."
Philippians 4:6-7 (NIV)

FAMILY FAITH IN ACTION

Option 1: Angel Wings of Encouragement (Craft)

Supplies: Paper, scissors, and markers.

1. Trace and cut out angel wings.
2. On each one, write a word or message of encouragement (hope, peace, "You are loved").
3. Hang or tape the wings in places where family members will see them this week.

Connection:
Just like Gabriel shared God's message with Mary, we can use kind words to lift others up and remind them that God is near.

Option 2: "Say Yes" Challenge (Action)

1. Each person thinks of one simple way to say "yes" to God today. It could be helping, sharing, or forgiving.
2. Write it down or share it aloud, then pray that God helps you do it joyfully.

Connection:
Mary's yes to God changed the world. Each small yes we give can shine His love in big ways.

PERSONAL REFLECTION

Before you pray, take a moment to write or draw:
- What's something God might be asking you to say "yes" to?

- What prayer request or need is on your heart tonight?

(Encourage each family member to write or share aloud if they'd like.)

FAMILY PRAYER TIME

Choose one person to lead the prayer tonight.
It can be as simple as thanking God for speaking to us through His Word or asking Him to help you trust Him like Mary did.

DAY 3 MARY'S SONG OF JOY LUKE 1:46-55

"My soul glorifies the Lord and my spirit rejoices in God my Savior." — Luke 1:46-47 (NIV)

BEFORE YOU BEGIN

Color in Day 3 on your Advent Tracker. Take a moment to think of one thing that made you smile today. Then read today's verse aloud, the same joyful words Mary sang when she realized that God was doing something amazing through her life.

THE READING - A SONG OF JOY AND FAITH

After hearing the angel's message, Mary visited her cousin Elizabeth. When they met, Mary couldn't hold her joy inside; she sang a song of praise, thanking God for keeping His promises.

Mary's song reminds us that joy isn't just about feeling happy, it's about trusting that God is good and faithful, even when life feels uncertain. Her heart overflowed with praise because she knew God's plan was full of hope.

Read Luke 1:46-55 together. As you read, listen for the reasons Mary gives for rejoicing in God.

FAMILY READ-ALOUD SUMMARY

Mary sang a song to praise God for His goodness. She thanked Him for choosing her and for keeping His promises to His people. Her joy came from knowing that God was with her and that His love never fails.

STUDY & REFLECTION ON LUKE 1:46-55

All suggestions are optional; the most important thing is interacting with God's Word and connecting with what He wants to show you today.

KEY THEMES

- True joy comes from knowing God, not from our circumstances.
- Gratitude grows when we remember what God has done.
- Worship is our response to God's goodness.

1. **Read the passage slowly** — Luke 1:46-55
Pause when you reach a line that makes you smile or gives you hope.

2. **Write or draw the verse or phrase in your Bible margin or journal.** Beside it, write one reason you can thank God today, big or small.

Add a doodle or sticker that reminds you of joy (a heart, sunshine, or smiley face).

3. **Make the connection** - Ask yourself: "What happens to my heart when I stop and thank God?" Write, draw, or talk about your answer together.

PRACTICAL APPLICATION

When you feel grumpy, tired, or discouraged, stop and think of one thing God has done for you, then thank Him for it.
- Mary's joy started with gratitude, and ours can too.

CHOOSE JOY!

TEACHING POINTS

1. Mary's joy came from her faith, not her situation. She praised God before seeing how His plan would unfold, showing us that joy is rooted in trust.
2. Her song reminds us that joy isn't something we wait for; it's something we choose when we focus on God's promises. Gratitude turns ordinary moments into worship.

SCRIPTURE CONNECTION

"Shout for joy to the Lord, all the earth. Worship the Lord with gladness; come before Him with joyful songs."
Psalm 100:1-2 (NIV)

FAMILY STUDY QUESTIONS

(Choose one or two to discuss together.)

1. Why do you think Mary sang a song instead of just saying thank you?
2. What's one thing that makes you want to thank or praise God today?
3. How can our family show joy together this week?

FAMILY FAITH IN ACTION

Option 1: Joy Jar (Family Gratitude Game)

Supplies: A jar, small papers, and markers.

1. Everyone writes one thing they're thankful for and places it in the jar.
2. Read them aloud as a family and thank God for each one.

Connection:
Mary's joy began with thankfulness. Every note in your jar is a little song of gratitude!

Option 2: Sing It Loud! (Action)

1. Turn to the lyrics page for "Joy to the World."
2. Gather as a family and sing together, loud, off-key, joyful, and full of heart!
3. When you're done, take a moment to talk about what the words mean to you.

Connection:
Joy isn't just a song, it's something we live. As you sing, let your joy shine the same way the angels did when they announced His birth!

Closing Prayer

PERSONAL REFLECTION

Before you pray, take a moment to write or draw:
- What's one thing that brought you joy today? It could be something you're thankful for, or something that reminded you of God's goodness.

(Encourage each family member to write or share aloud if they'd like.)

FAMILY PRAYER TIME

Choose one person to lead the prayer tonight.
It can be as simple as thanking God for the joy He gives or asking Him to help you share that joy with others.

"JOY TO THE WORLD"

Lyrics by Isaac Watts (1719); Music by Lowell Mason (1848).
Public Domain.

Verse 1
Joy to the world! the Lord is come;
Let earth receive her King;
Let every heart prepare Him room,
And heaven and nature sing,
And heaven and nature sing,
And heaven, and heaven, and nature sing.

Verse 2
Joy to the earth! the Savior reigns;
Let men their songs employ;
While fields and floods, rocks, hills, and plains
Repeat the sounding joy,
Repeat the sounding joy,
Repeat, repeat, the sounding joy.

Verse 3
No more let sins and sorrows grow,
Nor thorns infest the ground;
He comes to make His blessings flow
Far as the curse is found,
Far as the curse is found,
Far as, far as, the curse is found.

Verse 4
He rules the world with truth and grace,
And makes the nations prove
The glories of His righteousness,
And wonders of His love,
And wonders of His love,
And wonders, wonders, of His love.

> What does it mean to make room for Jesus in your heart or home this Christmas?

> How can our family help spread joy to others, like the song says?

> What part of the song makes you feel the most joy, and why?

With God all things are possible

faith • joy • hope

DAY 4   JOSEPH'S DREAM   MATTHEW 1:18-25

"Joseph son of David, do not be afraid to take Mary home as your wife, because what is conceived in her is from the Holy Spirit." — Matthew 1:20 (NIV)

BEFORE YOU BEGIN

Color in Day 4 on your Advent Tracker. Take a quiet moment to think about a time you had to make a hard decision. Then read today's verse aloud and remember, when God asks us to trust Him, He always provides peace and direction.

THE READING - TRUSTING GOD'S PLAN

Joseph loved Mary, but when he found out she was expecting a child, he didn't know what to do. Before he could act, God sent an angel to him in a dream. The angel told Joseph not to be afraid, that the baby was from the Holy Spirit, and that he should name Him *Jesus*, because He would save people from their sins.

Joseph woke up and immediately obeyed. He didn't argue or wait for more proof. He trusted God's message and did what was right, even though it wasn't easy.

Read Matthew 1:18-25 together and listen for how Joseph shows faith through action.

FAMILY READ-ALOUD SUMMARY

An angel told Joseph in a dream that Mary's baby was from God. Joseph listened, trusted, and obeyed. He showed that faith means following God even when life feels confusing.

STUDY & REFLECTION ON MATTHEW 1:18-25

All suggestions are optional; the most important thing is interacting with God's Word and connecting with what He wants to show you today.

1. **Read the passage slowly** — Matthew 1:18-25. Pause when you read something that shows trust or obedience.

2. **Write or draw the verse or phrase in your Bible margin or journal.** Under it, draw a moon or pillow to symbolize Joseph's dream, or a heart to show obedience.

3. **Make the connection** - Ask yourself: "When has God asked me to do something hard or unexpected?" Write, draw, or talk about your answer together.

KEY THEMES

- God's plans often look different from ours.
- Faith shows through obedience.
- Trust grows when we listen to God's voice.

PRACTICAL APPLICATION

This week, look for one small way to obey God right away, maybe helping someone, being honest, or forgiving quickly.

- Faith grows stronger each time we choose obedience.

GOD, THANK YOU FOR GUIDING ME WHEN LIFE FEELS UNCERTAIN.

TEACHING POINTS

1. Joseph's story reminds us that obedience is an act of faith. Even when Joseph didn't understand everything, he chose to trust what God said.
2. True faith doesn't always need the full picture, just a willing heart. God honors those who listen and follow Him with courage.

SCRIPTURE CONNECTION

"Trust in the Lord with all your heart and lean not on your own understanding; in all your ways submit to Him, and He will make your paths straight." — Proverbs 3:5-6 (NIV)

FAMILY STUDY QUESTIONS

(Choose one or two to discuss together.)

1. Why do you think Joseph trusted the angel's message?
2. How can we show faith by our actions this week?
3. What helps you listen for God's voice when you're unsure?

FAMILY FAITH IN ACTION

Option 1: Dream Notes (Craft + Encouragement)

Supplies: Small papers, pens, envelopes, or a jar.

1. Each family member writes one hope, prayer, or dream for the season.
2. Fold and place them in the jar.
3. Pray together, asking God to guide each dream according to His plan.

Connection:
Joseph's dream brought peace and direction. God still guides us when we listen and trust Him.

Option 2: Quick to Obey Challenge (Action)

1. After reading and praying together, think of one small thing you can do right now that shows obedience or kindness. (It could be helping clean up, sending an encouraging message, or forgiving someone who upset you.)
2. Once you've done it, thank God for giving you the courage to act in faith.

Connection:
Faith isn't just believing; it's trusting God enough to take action right away.

PERSONAL REFLECTION

Before you pray, take a moment to write or draw:
- One area of your life where you need to trust God more.
- Ask Him to help you obey even when you don't see the whole picture.

(Encourage each family member to write or share aloud if they'd like.)

FAMILY PRAYER TIME

Choose one person to lead the prayer tonight.
It can be as simple as thanking God for guiding us when things are uncertain or asking Him to help us trust His plan, like Joseph did.

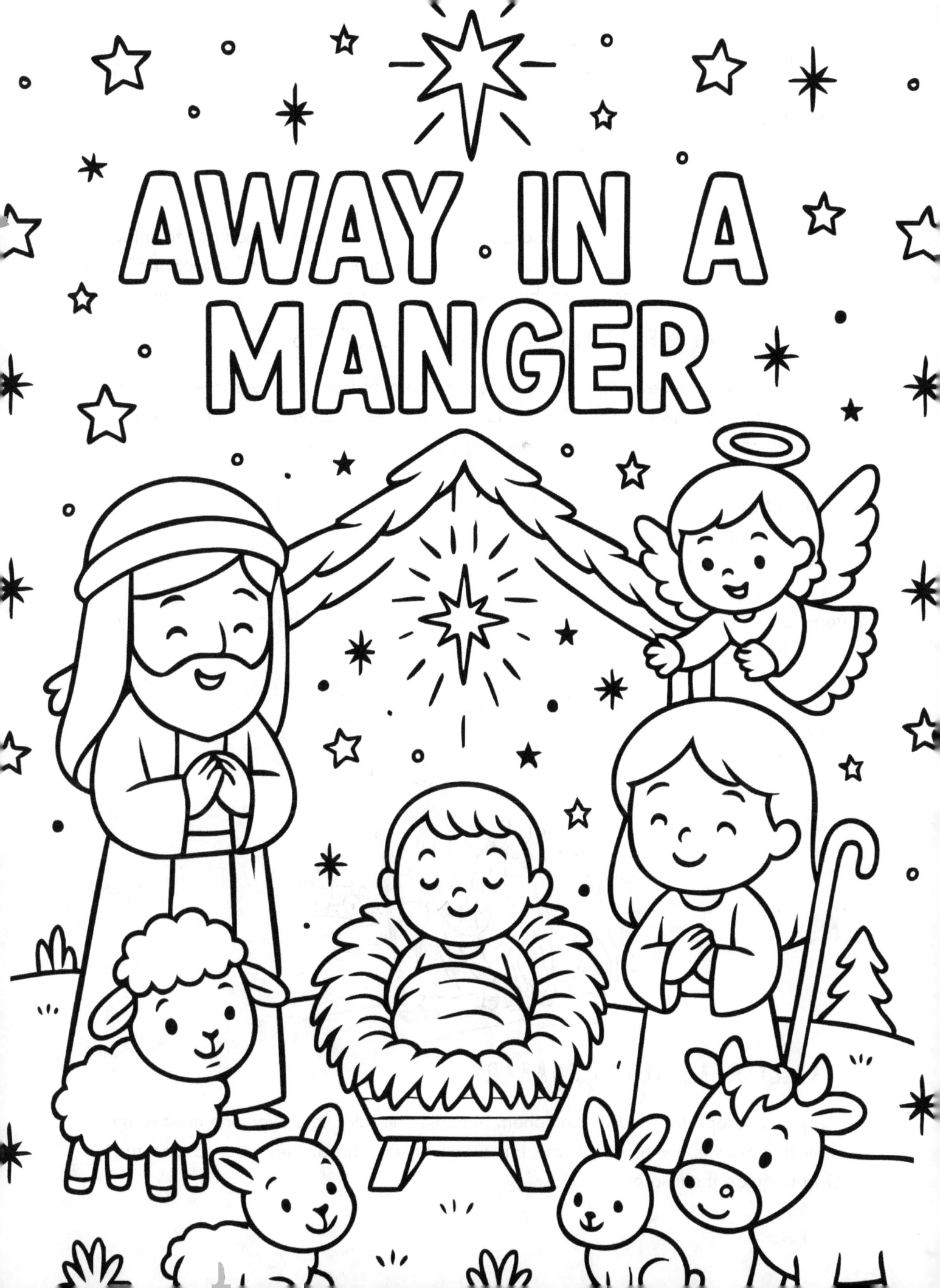

DAY 5 — THE JOURNEY BEGINS — LUKE 2:1-5

"So Joseph also went up from the town of Nazareth in Galilee to Judea, to Bethlehem the town of David." — Luke 2:4 (NIV)

BEFORE YOU BEGIN

Color in Day 5 on your Advent Tracker. Before reading, take a moment to imagine packing for a long trip. What would you bring? Now think of Mary and Joseph, traveling far from home with trust and hope, believing God was with them the entire way.

THE READING - FOLLOWING WHERE GOD LEADS

The emperor ordered everyone to return to their hometowns for a census, so Joseph and Mary had to travel to Bethlehem, a journey of almost 90 miles. It wasn't an easy trip, especially for Mary, who was expecting a baby.

But step by step, they kept going. Their faith didn't depend on comfort or understanding. They trusted that every step brought them closer to what God had promised.

Read Luke 2:1-5 together, and picture what that journey might have been like: dusty roads, tired feet, and hearts full of trust.

FAMILY READ-ALOUD SUMMARY

Mary and Joseph traveled to Bethlehem because the ruler said everyone must return to their hometowns. Even though the trip was long and hard, they obeyed and trusted God to guide them safely.

STUDY & REFLECTION ON LUKE 2:1-5

All suggestions are optional; the most important thing is interacting with God's Word and connecting with what He wants to show you today.

1. **Read the passage slowly** — Luke 2:1-5. Imagine the journey to Bethlehem, how might it have felt for Mary and Joseph?

2. **Write or draw a picture of a path or road in your Bible margin or journal.** Under it, write a short thought or prayer about what your own "faith journey" feels like right now.
(Example: "God, help me keep walking with You, even when the road feels long.")

3. **Make the connection** - Ask yourself: "What journey am I on right now?" Write your thoughts, draw a symbol of faith for your journey, or talk about your answer together.

TEACHING POINTS

1. Mary and Joseph didn't know what challenges they'd face, but they moved forward because they believed in God's promise. Their story reminds us that God's plan often begins with a single step of faith.
2. Even when the road feels long, God's presence travels with us. Trusting Him doesn't remove every struggle; it gives us strength to keep walking.

FAMILY STUDY QUESTIONS

(Choose one or two to discuss together.)

1. What helps you keep going when something feels hard?
2. How can we remind each other that God is with us every day?

KEY THEMES

- Obedience sometimes means taking a hard path.
- God is with us wherever we go.
- Faith means trusting one step at a time.

PRACTICAL APPLICATION

When something feels hard or uncertain today, whisper:

"GOD, WALK WITH ME."

That simple prayer reminds your heart that you're never traveling alone.

SCRIPTURE CONNECTION

"The Lord Himself goes before you and will be with you; He will never leave you nor forsake you. Do not be afraid; do not be discouraged."
— Deuteronomy 31:8 (NIV)

FAMILY FAITH IN ACTION

Option 1: "God Is With Us" Doorway Reminder (Craft)

Supplies: Paper, tape, and markers.

1. Write "God is with us wherever we go" on a paper sign.
2. Decorate it and tape it above a doorway in your home.
3. Every time you pass through it this week, say, "God is with me."

Connection:
Mary and Joseph's journey began with trust. This reminder helps your family carry that same faith wherever you go.

Option 2: The Family Path (Action)

1. Take a short walk together, even just around your home or yard.
2. As you walk, talk about what it means to trust God on life's journey.

If you can't go outside, trace a path on paper and write prayers along the road.

Connection:
Every step you take can remind you that God is walking beside you.

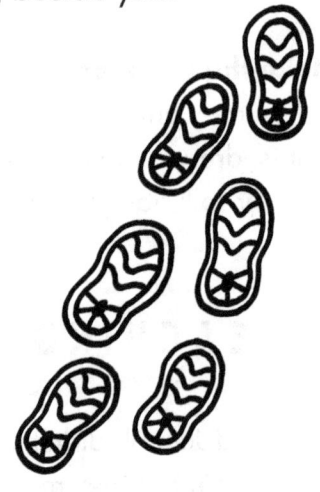

PERSONAL REFLECTION

Before you pray, take a moment to write or draw:
- One way you've seen God walk with you this week.
- Thank Him for being close, even on difficult days.

(Encourage each family member to write or share aloud if they'd like.)

FAMILY PRAYER TIME

Choose one person to lead the prayer tonight.
It can be as simple as thanking God for walking with us each day or asking Him to give us strength for the journey ahead.

THE STAR OF BETHLEHEM ☆

The Star of Bethlehem guided the wise men to Jesus, a symbol of God's light in the darkness.

Some believe it may have been a rare alignment of planets, but believers know it was part of God's perfect plan.

GOD'S LIGHT STILL LEADS US TO JESUS.

Quick Activity: Draw or color stars around the page to represent the ways God has guided your family this year.

The star reminds us to look up; God's promises always shine, even when the world feels dark.

DAY 6   THE STAR OF BETHLEHEM   MATTHEW 2:1-2

"We saw His star when it rose and have come to worship Him." — Matthew 2:2 (NIV)

BEFORE YOU BEGIN

Color in Day 6 on your Advent Tracker and take a moment to look up at the night sky, or, if it's daytime or cloudy, open a short starry-night video or background on YouTube. As you watch the stars shine, imagine the special light that led the wise men to Jesus, a sign of hope that still shines for us today.

THE READING - A LIGHT TO LEAD THE WAY

Far away, wise men saw a new star in the sky. They knew it meant something wonderful had happened, the Savior had been born. They began a long journey, following the light, determined to find Jesus and worship Him.

God used that star to guide them, just as He guides us through His Word and His Spirit. Sometimes we can't see the whole path ahead, but like the wise men, we can trust the light God gives for each step.

Read Matthew 2:1-2 together. Talk about what it means to "follow the light" in your own lives.

FAMILY READ-ALOUD SUMMARY

Wise men from far away saw a special star shining in the sky. They followed it to find baby Jesus and to bring Him gifts and worship. God used the star to lead them, just like He leads us with His truth and love.

STUDY & REFLECTION ON MATTHEW 2:1-2

All suggestions are optional; the most important thing is interacting with God's Word and connecting with what He wants to show you today.

1. **Read the passage slowly** — Matthew 2:1-2. Pause when you reach a word or phrase that makes you think about light or direction.

2. **Write or draw a bright star in your Bible margin or journal.** Under it, write a short prayer about something you want God to guide you in. (Example: "God, please show me Your light when I don't know what to do.")

3. **Make the connection** - Ask yourself: "How can I be a light for someone else?" Write your thoughts, create a small symbol of light near your verse, or talk about your answer together.

KEY THEMES

- God always provides light to guide us.
- True wisdom means following where God leads.
- Worship begins with seeking Jesus.

TEACHING POINTS

1. The wise men didn't know exactly where they were going, they just knew Who they were looking for. Their faith moved them to act.
2. The star reminds us that God's light never fades, and when we follow His leading, it always brings us closer to Jesus.
3. Even in dark or uncertain times, God's truth points the way, one step at a time.

PRACTICAL APPLICATION

If something feels confusing today, pause and pray:

"GOD, BE MY LIGHT."

Let that prayer remind you that His guidance is steady, even when you can't see the whole path.

SCRIPTURE CONNECTION

"Your word is a lamp for my feet, a light on my path." — Psalm 119:105 (NIV)

FAMILY STUDY QUESTIONS

(Choose one or two to discuss together.)

1. Why do you think God used a star to guide the wise men?
2. What helps you feel close to God's light when life feels dark?
3. How can our family shine God's light to others this week?

FAMILY FAITH IN ACTION

Option 1: Shine Your Light (Craft or Action)
Supplies: Flashlight or small LED candle.

1. Turn off the lights in the room.
2. One person turns on the light and slowly moves it around.
3. Talk about how even one light can change darkness.
4. End by thanking God for being the Light of the World.

Connection:
Just as the star guided the wise men, God's light helps us find our way and reminds us to shine for others.

Option 2: Star Trail Prayer (Creative Activity)
Supplies: Paper, scissors, pencil or markers, and optional glitter or stickers.

1. Draw or print a large star on paper.
2. Inside the star, write the names of people you want God to guide or bless this week.
3. Decorate your star with color, sparkle, or light to make it shine.
4. Pray together as a family for each name you wrote inside the star.

Connection:
The star led the wise men to Jesus; your prayers can help lead hearts closer to Him, too.

Closing Prayer

PERSONAL REFLECTION

Before you pray, take a moment to write or draw:
- One place in your life where you want God's light to shine brighter.
- Thank Him for being your constant guide.

(Encourage each family member to write or share aloud if they'd like.)

FAMILY PRAYER TIME

Choose one person to lead the prayer tonight.
It can be as simple as thanking God for being our light or asking Him to help us shine His love to others.

DAY 7 NO ROOM AT THE INN LUKE 2:6-7

"While they were there, the time came for the baby to be born, and she gave birth to her firstborn, a son." — Luke 2:6-7 (NIV)

BEFORE YOU BEGIN

Color in Day 7 on your Advent Tracker. Then take a quiet moment to think of what "home" means to you, not just the place, but the feeling. As you read today's verse, imagine Mary and Joseph arriving in Bethlehem, tired and searching for a place to rest, only to find that every room was full.

THE READING - MAKING ROOM FOR JESUS

When Mary and Joseph reached Bethlehem, there was no place for them to stay. Every inn was crowded with travelers coming for the census. But even without a warm bed or fancy room, God made a way; a humble stable became the birthplace of the King of Kings.

This moment reminds us that Jesus doesn't need perfect circumstances to enter our lives. He just needs a willing heart and an open space.

Read Luke 2:6-7 together. As you read, imagine what that stable might have looked like: simple, quiet, and filled with God's presence.

FAMILY READ-ALOUD SUMMARY

Mary and Joseph couldn't find a place to stay, so baby Jesus was born in a stable. Even though it was simple, it became the most special place in the world because God's Son was there.

STUDY & REFLECTION ON LUKE 2:6-7

All suggestions are optional; the most important thing is interacting with God's Word and connecting with what He wants to show you today.

1. **Read the passage slowly** — Luke 2:6-7. Picture the scene: the stable, the manger, the quiet night.

2. **Write or draw a small heart or open door in your Bible margin or journal.** Under it, write a short prayer about making space for Jesus in your life. (Example: "Jesus, help me make room for You in my heart every day.")

3. **Make the connection** - Ask yourself: "What fills up my time or heart and makes it hard to make space for God?" Write your thoughts, draw something that reminds you of peace and warmth, or talk about your answer together.

TEACHING POINTS

1. The world didn't make room for Jesus when He came, but we can.
2. God's plan wasn't stopped by a full inn or an unexpected setting. He turned an ordinary stable into a holy place because His presence changes everything.
3. When we make room for Jesus in our lives, through kindness, prayer, or love, He fills our hearts with peace that lasts longer than any comfort we could find on our own.

FAMILY STUDY QUESTIONS

(Choose one or two to discuss together.)

1. Why do you think Jesus was born in such a simple place?
2. What does it mean to "make room" for God in our lives?
3. How can our family make space for Jesus this Christmas season?

KEY THEMES

- God works through humble beginnings.
- Making space for Jesus means opening our hearts.
- Small, simple moments can hold great meaning.

PRACTICAL APPLICATION

Today, look for a small way to make space for someone, let a sibling go first, listen to someone who needs to talk, or share something you have.

EVERY TIME WE MAKE ROOM FOR OTHERS, WE MAKE ROOM FOR JESUS.

SCRIPTURE CONNECTION

"Here I am! I stand at the door and knock. If anyone hears my voice and opens the door, I will come in and eat with that person, and they with me."
— Revelation 3:20 (NIV)

FAMILY FAITH IN ACTION

Option 1: The Welcome Space (Simple Visual Action)

1. As a family, choose one small spot in your home, it could be a corner, a table, or even your Christmas tree area, and call it your "Welcome Space."
2. Say together, "Jesus, we make room for You here."
3. You can leave a small reminder there this week, a candle, ornament, or drawing, to symbolize your invitation for Him to dwell in your home.

Connection:
Mary and Joseph couldn't find a room, but you're inviting Jesus into your home and heart.

Option 2: A Kind Word for Someone New (Action)

1. Each person chooses someone outside your immediate family, a neighbor, teacher, classmate, or relative, and sends or says one kind word to remind them they matter.
2. It could be a text, a note, or a smile with meaning.

Connection:
When we make space in our hearts for others, we make space for Jesus too.

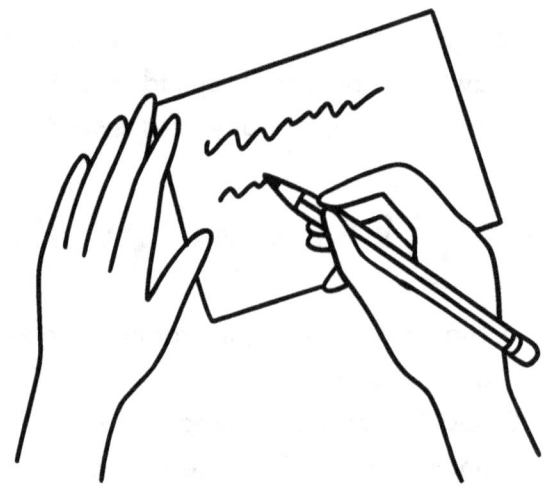

PERSONAL REFLECTION

Before you pray, take a moment to write or draw:
- Write or draw one way you can make room for Jesus this week, in your time, your heart, or your actions.

(Encourage each family member to write or share aloud if they'd like.)

FAMILY PRAYER TIME

Choose one person to lead the prayer tonight.
It can be as simple as thanking God for always making a place for us or asking Him to help us make space for Him in our hearts.

DAY 8   SHEPHERDS IN THE NIGHT   LUKE 2:8-12

"Do not be afraid. I bring you good news that will cause great joy for all the people."
— Luke 2:10 (NIV)

BEFORE YOU BEGIN

Color in Day 8 on your Advent Tracker. If you can, step outside for a moment and look at the night sky, or open a "night stars" video on YouTube. Take a deep breath and imagine what the shepherds saw that night: the quiet field, the glowing sky, and the angels' song of joy.

THE READING - GOOD NEWS FOR EVERYONE

That night, shepherds were watching their flocks when an angel appeared and lit up the sky. The angel told them not to be afraid, because a Savior had been born in Bethlehem!

The shepherds were the first to hear the news of Jesus' birth. Even though they were ordinary people doing everyday work, God chose them to be messengers of His joy.

Read Luke 2:8-12 together. As you read, imagine how the shepherds felt when heaven touched earth.

FAMILY READ-ALOUD SUMMARY

While they were watching their sheep, the shepherds saw an angel shining in the night sky. The angel told them that Jesus had been born and that they could go and see Him. The good news was for everyone, even ordinary people like them.

STUDY & REFLECTION ON LUKE 2:8-12

All suggestions are optional; the most important thing is interacting with God's Word and connecting with what He wants to show you today.

1. **Read the passage slowly** — Luke 2:8-12. Picture the dark sky filling with light.

2. **Write or draw what you think the shepherds might have felt in that moment in your Bible margin or journal.** Under it, write a short prayer about sharing joy or good news with others. (Example: "God, help me tell others about You with joy and courage.")

3. **Make the connection** - Ask yourself: "What good news has God given me to share?" Write, draw, or talk about your answer together.

KEY THEMES

- God brings good news to ordinary people.
- The message of Jesus is for everyone.
- Joy grows when we share it.

PRACTICAL APPLICATION

This week, share one piece of good news, big or small, with someone. It could be a story of kindness, a blessing, or something God has done for you.

GOOD NEWS GROWS WHEN WE SHARE IT!

TEACHING POINTS

1. The shepherds weren't famous or rich, but God trusted them with the best news in history. That shows us something important. God values every heart that listens.
2. The good news of Jesus isn't just something we keep to ourselves; it's meant to be shared. Just like the shepherds ran to tell others, we can share His love in small, joyful ways.

SCRIPTURE CONNECTION

"How beautiful on the mountains are the feet of those who bring good news, who proclaim peace, who bring good tidings." — Isaiah 52:7 (NIV)

FAMILY STUDY QUESTIONS

(Choose one or two to discuss together.)

1. Why do you think God told the shepherds first?
2. What does "good news" mean to you?
3. How can we share God's joy together as a family?

FAMILY FAITH IN ACTION

Option 1: "Good News Echo" (Joy Game)

1. Each person takes turns saying one thing they're thankful for or something good that happened recently.
2. After each person shares, the rest of the family echoes together:
   "Good news! God is good!"
3. Keep going until everyone has shared, big things or small things alike.

Connection:
Just like the shepherds shared the good news of Jesus' birth, you're spreading joy right where you are.

Option 2: "Share the Joy" (Creative Action)

Supplies: Paper, markers, or sticky notes.

1. Write short messages of joy or encouragement, like:
   "You are loved!"
   "God is with you!"
   "Good news, Jesus brings joy!"
2. Place them around your home, in lunchboxes, or on mirrors to surprise someone later.

Connection:
The shepherds couldn't keep the good news to themselves, and neither should we! These simple notes are your way of sharing God's joy with others.

PERSONAL REFLECTION

Before you pray, take a moment to write or draw:
- Write or draw one piece of "good news" that made you smile this week, something God has done, or a small blessing you noticed.
- Underneath, write a short prayer of thanks.

(Encourage each family member to write or share aloud if they'd like.)

FAMILY PRAYER TIME

Choose one person to lead the prayer tonight.
It can be as simple as thanking God for the good news He brings or asking Him to help your family share His joy with others this week.

DAY 9 — A HEAVENLY CHOIR — LUKE 2:13-14

"Suddenly a great company of the heavenly host appeared with the angel, praising God and saying, 'Glory to God in the highest heaven, and on earth peace to those on whom His favor rests.'" — Luke 2:13-14 (NIV)

BEFORE YOU BEGIN

Color in Day 9 on your Advent Tracker. Then, before reading, take a deep breath and imagine the night sky lighting up with thousands of angels singing all at once. Heaven was celebrating, and the world would never be the same again.

THE READING - HEAVEN SINGS, EARTH REJOICES

After the angel shared the good news with the shepherds, the sky filled with a heavenly choir. Thousands of angels praised God, singing about peace and joy for everyone who would receive Jesus.

That night, heaven and earth sang the same song, one of praise and hope. God was keeping His promise, and His love was breaking through the darkness.

Read Luke 2:13-14 together. Imagine what it must have sounded like, the most beautiful song ever sung.

FAMILY READ-ALOUD SUMMARY

The sky filled with angels singing praises to God. They celebrated the birth of Jesus and announced peace on earth. The shepherds heard heaven's song, and we can still sing it today.

STUDY & REFLECTION ON LUKE 2:13-14

All suggestions are optional; the most important thing is interacting with God's Word and connecting with what He wants to show you today.

KEY THEMES

- Worship is our response to God's goodness.
- God's peace is for everyone.
- Heaven celebrates when God's promises are fulfilled.

1. **Read the passage slowly** — Luke 2:13-14. Close your eyes and imagine the angels' song echoing across the sky.

2. **Write or draw musical notes or a song title that makes you think of God's peace and joy in your Bible margin or journal.** Under it, write a short prayer of praise. (Example: "God, You are worthy of all my praise. Thank You for bringing peace to my heart.")

3. **Make the connection** - Ask yourself: "What helps me feel God's peace?" Write, draw, or talk about your answer together.

PRACTICAL APPLICATION

Turn on your favorite worship or Christmas song today.

- As you listen, thank God for sending Jesus and for bringing peace to your heart.

"GOD, THANK YOU FOR THE SONG OF THE ANGELS. HELP MY LIFE BE A SONG OF PRAISE TO YOU."

TEACHING POINTS

1. The angels didn't just announce good news; they sang it. Their worship reminds us that joy leads to praise. When we sing, pray, or thank God, we join the same chorus that filled the sky that night.
2. God's peace doesn't mean everything is perfect; it means we can rest knowing He is in control. That's why the angels sang "Glory to God in the highest."

SCRIPTURE CONNECTION

"Come, let us sing for joy to the Lord; let us shout aloud to the Rock of our salvation. Let us come before Him with thanksgiving and extol Him with music and song." — Psalm 95:1-2 (NIV)

FAMILY STUDY QUESTIONS

(Choose one or two to discuss together.)

1. Why do you think the angels sang instead of just speaking?
2. What does "peace on earth" mean to you?
3. How can our family worship God together this week?

FAMILY FAITH IN ACTION

Option 1: "Heaven's Song" (Family Sing-Along)

1. Play or sing *"Hark! The Herald Angels Sing"* together.
2. Afterward, talk about what the words mean, especially "peace on earth."
3. If you have small children, let them create hand motions or dance to the song!

Connection:
When we sing about Jesus, we're joining the same song the angels sang that night.

💡 The lyrics for *"Hark! The Herald Angels Sing"* are available on the next page so your family can read or sing along together.

Option 2: "Peace Postcards" (Creative Action)

Supplies: Blank cards or paper, crayons or markers.

1. Create "Peace Postcards" with messages like:

> "Peace on earth begins with love."
> "God's peace is for everyone."

2. Decorate them and give them to friends, teachers, or neighbors this week.

Connection:
Just like the angels shared peace through song, your family can share peace through kindness and words of hope.

PERSONAL REFLECTION

Before you pray, take a moment to write or draw:
- Write or draw one way you can bring peace into your home this week, through words, actions, or prayer. (Example: "I can listen more when someone is upset.")

(Encourage each family member to write or share aloud if they'd like.)

FAMILY PRAYER TIME

Choose one person to lead the prayer tonight.
It can be as simple as thanking God for the song of peace the angels sang or asking Him to fill your family with that same peace today.

"HARK! THE HERALD ANGELS SING"

Lyrics by Charles Wesley (1739); Music by Felix Mendelssohn (1840s). Public Domain.

Verse 1
Hark! the herald angels sing,
Glory to the newborn King;
Peace on earth, and mercy mild,
God and sinners reconciled.
Joyful, all ye nations, rise,
Join the triumph of the skies;
With th'angelic host proclaim,
Christ is born in Bethlehem!
Hark! the herald angels sing,
Glory to the newborn King!

Verse 2
Christ, by highest heaven adored,
Christ, the everlasting Lord;
Late in time behold Him come,
Offspring of the Virgin's womb.
Veiled in flesh, the Godhead see;
Hail, th'incarnate Deity!
Pleased, as man, with men to dwell,
Jesus, our Emmanuel!
Hark! the herald angels sing,
Glory to the newborn King!

Verse 3
Hail! the Heaven-born Prince of Peace!
Hail, the Son of Righteousness!
Light and life to all He brings,
Risen with healing in His wings.
Mild He lays His glory by,
Born that man no more may die;
Born to raise the sons of earth,
Born to give them second birth.
Hark! the herald angels sing,
Glory to the newborn King!

> What does 'Peace on earth' mean to you today?

> Why do you think the angels sang 'Glory to the newborn King'?

> Which line reminds you most of God's love?

THE CHRISTMAS TREE ☆

- Evergreen trees stay green all year long, they remind us of God's never-ending love.
- The ornaments symbolize blessings and gifts from God.
- The star on top reminds us of the star that led the wise men to Jesus.
- The lights represent Jesus, the Light of the World.

GOD'S LOVE NEVER FADES, IT'S ALIVE FOREVER, JUST LIKE THE EVERGREEN TREE.

DAY 10   THE CHRISTMAS TREE   PSALM 1:3; JOHN 3:16

"That person is like a tree planted by streams of water, which yields its fruit in season and whose leaf does not wither—whatever they do prospers." — Psalm 1:3 (NIV)

BEFORE YOU BEGIN

Color in Day 10 on your Advent Tracker. Take a moment to look at your Christmas tree (or a photo of one). Notice how it shines with lights and ornaments, a symbol of life, beauty, and joy. Today, you'll discover how the evergreen tree reminds us of God's everlasting love.

THE READING - A SYMBOL OF EVERLASTING LIFE

The Christmas tree isn't just a decoration; it's a reminder of life that never fades. Evergreen trees stay green all year long, no matter the season, just like God's love never changes.

The Bible says that those who stay close to God are like a tree planted by water, strong, rooted, and full of life. And through Jesus, God gave us the greatest gift of all, eternal life.

Read Psalm 1:3 and John 3:16 together. Talk about what it means to have "everlasting life" in Christ.

FAMILY READ-ALOUD SUMMARY

The evergreen tree stays alive and full of color all year long. It reminds us that God's love never fades and that life with Jesus lasts forever.

STUDY & REFLECTION ON PSALM 1:3 AND JOHN 3:16

All suggestions are optional; the most important thing is interacting with God's Word and connecting with what He wants to show you today.

1. **Read the passage slowly** — Psalm 1:3 and John 3:16.

2. **Write or draw a simple tree with strong roots in your Bible margin or journal.** Under it, write one way you can stay rooted in God this week. (Example: "God, help my faith grow strong and stay rooted in You.")

3. **Make the connection** - Ask yourself: "What helps my faith grow?" Write, draw, or talk about your answer together.

KEY THEMES

- God's love is everlasting.
- Our faith should stay rooted and strong like a tree.
- Jesus is the greatest gift, everlasting life through Him.

PRACTICAL APPLICATION

Find one way to "light up" someone's day, through encouragement, patience, or a small act of generosity.

- Let your kindness shine like the lights on the Christmas tree.

WHEN OUR ROOTS GROW DEEP IN GOD'S LOVE, WE CAN STAND STRONG.

TEACHING POINTS

1. Every branch of the Christmas tree points upward, reminding us to keep our eyes on God.
2. Its evergreen color stands for life that doesn't fade, and the lights remind us that Jesus is the Light of the World.
3. When we keep our roots in God's Word, our hearts stay full of peace, even in hard seasons.

SCRIPTURE CONNECTION

"So then, just as you received Christ Jesus as Lord, continue to live your lives in Him, rooted and built up in Him, strengthened in the faith as you were taught, and overflowing with thankfulness."
— Colossians 2:6–7 (NIV)

FAMILY STUDY QUESTIONS

(Choose one or two to discuss together.)

1. Every Christmas tree points upward. What do you think that teaches us about where our hope comes from?
2. How does the tree remind us of God's love that never fades or changes?
3. What are some ways we can stay rooted in faith and let God's light shine through us all year long?

FAMILY FAITH IN ACTION

Option 1: "Blessing Ornaments" (Creative Action)

Supplies: Paper, scissors, string, markers.

1. Cut out small paper ornament shapes.
2. On each, write something you're thankful for, then hang them on your tree (or a wall).

Connection:
The Christmas tree is full of life, just like our hearts when we remember God's blessings.

Option 2: Decorate the Tree of Blessings" (Creative Action)

Supplies: Crayons, stickers. or markers.

1. Use the tree on the next page.
2. Decorate it with crayons, stickers, or markers.
3. For every ornament you draw or color, say something you're thankful for.

Connection:
Each ornament becomes a reminder that God's love never fades and His blessings fill our lives year-round.

PERSONAL REFLECTION

Before you pray, take a moment to write or draw:
- Write or draw one blessing that reminds you of God's everlasting love. (Example: "God, thank You for never changing, Your love keeps me strong.")

(Encourage each family member to write or share aloud if they'd like.)

FAMILY PRAYER TIME

Choose one person to lead the prayer tonight.
It can be as simple as thanking God for His everlasting love or asking Him to help your family stay rooted in faith.

TREE OF GRATITUDE

DAY 11   THE GOOD NEWS SPREADS   LUKE 2:15-18

"When they had seen Him, they spread the word concerning what had been told them about this Child." — Luke 2:17 (NIV)

BEFORE YOU BEGIN

Color in Day 11 on your Advent Tracker. Take a deep breath and smile, it's time to celebrate the moment the shepherds couldn't keep quiet about! They had seen Jesus, and their hearts overflowed with joy.

THE READING - JOY MEANT TO BE SHARED

After the angels left, the shepherds hurried to Bethlehem and found Mary, Joseph, and baby Jesus, just as the angel had said. They were so amazed that they couldn't keep the news to themselves! They told everyone what they had seen, and people were filled with wonder.

Read Luke 2:15-18 together. Talk about what it feels like to be so excited about something that you have to share it.

FAMILY READ-ALOUD SUMMARY

The shepherds saw baby Jesus and couldn't wait to tell others. Everyone who heard their story was amazed! When something fills your heart with joy, it's meant to be shared, just like the good news of Jesus.

STUDY & REFLECTION ON LUKE 2:15-18

All suggestions are optional; the most important thing is interacting with God's Word and connecting with what He wants to show you today.

1. **Read the passage slowly** — Luke 2:15-18.

2. **Write or draw something that brings you joy, a moment, person, or gift from God in your Bible margin or journal.** Under it, write how you could share that joy with someone else this week.

3. **Make the connection** - Ask yourself: "Who might need to hear good news today?" Write, draw, or talk about your answer together.

KEY THEMES

- Good news is meant to be shared.
- Our joy grows when we tell others about Jesus.
- Sharing faith can be simple, it starts with love.

PRACTICAL APPLICATION

Find one way to share joy today: send a kind message, give a compliment, or pray for someone.

TEACHING POINTS

1. The shepherds didn't wait; they went right away to share what they saw.
2. You don't need to be a preacher to share good news.
3. Sometimes, it's as simple as showing kindness, speaking encouragement, or living in a way that points others to Jesus.
4. When we share what God has done for us, others get to see His light through us.

YOUR WORDS AND ACTIONS CAN SPREAD GOOD NEWS, TOO!

SCRIPTURE CONNECTION

"Let your light shine before others, that they may see your good deeds and glorify your Father in heaven." — Matthew 5:16 (NIV)

FAMILY STUDY QUESTIONS

(Choose one or two to discuss together.)

1. Why do you think the shepherds told everyone what they saw?
2. How do you feel when you share something exciting?
3. What's one way our family can share God's love this week?

FAMILY FAITH IN ACTION

Option 1: "Pass the Praise" (Joy Game)

1. Sit in a circle.
2. One person says something good God has done ("God helped me be brave today!"). Then points to someone else to continue the praise chain.
3. Keep passing it until everyone has shared at least once!

Connection:
Sharing good news builds joy, just like the shepherds spreading their excitement about Jesus.

Option 2: "Thankful Notes" (Creative Action)

Supplies: Paper, pens, blank cards, or sticky notes.

1. Write a short "I'm thankful for you" note and place it somewhere for someone to find at home, school, or work.

Connection:
Every word of kindness is a way to share God's love. Small notes can spread big joy.

Closing Prayer

PERSONAL REFLECTION

Before you pray, take a moment to write or draw:
Write or draw one way you shared joy today (or plan to). (Example: "I thanked my teacher," or "I prayed for my friend.")

(Encourage each family member to write or share aloud if they'd like.)

FAMILY PRAYER TIME

Choose one person to lead the prayer tonight.
It can be as simple as thanking God for giving us good news to share and asking Him to help your family spread His love through your words and actions.

What Child is this?

DAY 12 — MARY TREASURES IT ALL — LUKE 2:19-20

"But Mary treasured up all these things and pondered them in her heart." — Luke 2:19 (NIV)

BEFORE YOU BEGIN

Color in Day 12 on your Advent Tracker. Find a quiet place, maybe near your tree or window. Take one deep breath and think about all you've learned so far in your Advent journey. This is a day to pause, reflect, and treasure what God has done, just like Mary did.

THE READING - QUIET WONDER

After the shepherds left, Mary sat quietly, thinking about everything that had happened. She remembered the angel's message, the journey to Bethlehem, the baby in her arms, and the joy of everyone who came to see Him. She didn't rush or speak; she simply treasured it all in her heart.

Read Luke 2:19-20 together. Talk about what it means to slow down and think deeply about what God is doing in your life.

FAMILY READ-ALOUD SUMMARY

Mary didn't need to say a word. She remembered all that God had done and quietly thanked Him in her heart. Sometimes, the best way to worship is to pause and treasure what He's already given us.

STUDY & REFLECTION ON LUKE 2:19-20

All suggestions are optional; the most important thing is interacting with God's Word and connecting with what He wants to show you today.

1. **Read the passage slowly** — Luke 2:19-20.

2. **Write or draw one thing you've learned or noticed about God so far in this Advent journey in your Bible margin or journal.**
(Example: "God always keeps His promises," or "God brings peace to ordinary people.")

3. **Make the connection** - Ask yourself: "What do I want to treasure in my heart this season?" Write, draw, or talk about your answer together.

KEY THEMES

- Reflection deepens gratitude.
- God works in quiet, ordinary moments.
- Treasuring what God has done strengthens faith.

PRACTICAL APPLICATION

Find a few quiet minutes today, turn off the music, the TV, and distractions.
- Sit together as a family and take turns saying one thing you're thankful for from this Advent journey so far.

SOMETIMES WORSHIP LOOKS LIKE SINGING, BUT SOMETIMES IT LOOKS LIKE SILENCE. SITTING STILL AND FEELING THANKFUL.

TEACHING POINTS

1. Mary's story reminds us that not every part of faith is loud or visible.
2. Some moments are meant to be pondered, to think, pray, and thank God silently.
3. We live in a busy world, but God still speaks in stillness.
4. When we pause to treasure what He's done, our hearts grow stronger in faith and peace.

SCRIPTURE CONNECTION

"Be still, and know that I am God."
— Psalm 46:10 (NIV)

FAMILY STUDY QUESTIONS

(Choose one or two to discuss together.)

1. Why do you think Mary stayed quiet instead of speaking?
2. What's one thing you've seen God do in your life this season?
3. How can we make more space to "treasure" what God has done?

FAMILY FAITH IN ACTION

Option 1: "Silent Praise" (Simple Action)

1. Set a timer for one minute.
2. Sit together quietly and think about Jesus.
3. After the timer ends, each person shares one word that came to mind: peace, joy, love, hope, etc.

Connection:
Even silence can be worship when our hearts are focused on God.

Option 2: "Heart of Gratitude" (Creative Action)
Supplies: Paper hearts (or cutouts), pens, markers.

1. Write or draw one thing you want to thank God for and place it in a jar, under your tree, or on the wall.
2. Idea: Label the jar "Our Family Treasures."

Connection:
Mary treasured God's goodness quietly. This jar helps your family treasure those blessings all season long.

PERSONAL REFLECTION

Before you pray, take a moment to write or draw:
Write or draw one thing you're grateful for that you hadn't noticed before today.
(Example: "I'm thankful for how God helps me feel calm when I'm worried.")

(Encourage each family member to write or share aloud if they'd like.)

FAMILY PRAYER TIME

Choose one person to lead the prayer tonight.
It can be as simple as thanking God for the quiet moments that help us feel His peace.

GOD'S PEOPLE WAITED AND WONDERED FOR GENERATIONS.

WHEN THE TIME WAS JUST RIGHT, JESUS CAME!

DAY 13   GOD'S PERFECT TIMING   GALATIANS 4:4-5

"But when the set time had fully come, God sent his Son, born of a woman, born under the law, to redeem those under the law, that we might receive adoption to sonship."
— Galatians 4:4-5 (NIV)

BEFORE YOU BEGIN

Color in Day 13 on your Advent Tracker. Gather close and think about all the pieces that had to come together for Jesus to be born. The people, the place, the promise. Today, you'll read how God's plan arrived at exactly the right moment in history.

THE READING - RIGHT ON TIME

Have you ever waited for something that felt like it would never happen? A prayer, a dream, or a promise.

God's people waited hundreds of years for the Savior. It may have seemed like He was silent, but He was working all along, setting the right time, the right place, and the right people in motion.

When the moment was perfect, Jesus was born. God wasn't late. He wasn't early. His plan arrived right on time.

Read Galatians 4:4-5 together. Talk about what it means that God sent Jesus at "the set time."

FAMILY READ-ALOUD SUMMARY

God's people waited and wondered for generations. When the time was just right, Jesus came, bringing hope, peace, and love to everyone who believes. Even when we don't understand what God is doing, we can trust that His timing is always perfect.

STUDY & REFLECTION ON GALATIANS 4:4-5

All suggestions are optional; the most important thing is interacting with God's Word and connecting with what He wants to show you today.

1. **Read the passage slowly** — Galatians 4:4-5.

2. **Write or draw a small clock, hourglass, or calendar in your Bible margin or journal.** Inside it, write one thing you're waiting for or hoping God will do.

3. **Make the connection** - Ask yourself: "How can I trust God while I wait?" Write, draw, or talk about your answer together.

KEY THEMES

- God's plans are never rushed or delayed.
- Waiting with faith shows trust in His perfect plan.
- Jesus came at the exact moment the world needed hope.

PRACTICAL APPLICATION

Writing a thank-you note to someone who has been patient and kind with you helps us remember that patience and grace reflect God's own heart.

THE WAY WE WAIT AND TREAT OTHERS WHILE WE WAIT SHOWS WHAT WE BELIEVE ABOUT GOD'S GOODNESS.

TEACHING POINTS

1. Every event leading to Jesus' birth was part of God's design; nothing was accidental.
2. God's "perfect timing" reminds us that His plans are worth waiting for, even when we don't understand the delay.
3. Our waiting seasons often prepare us for what's ahead, just like the world was being prepared for Jesus.

SCRIPTURE CONNECTION

"He has made everything beautiful in its time." — Ecclesiastes 3:11 (NIV)

FAMILY STUDY QUESTIONS

(Choose one or two to discuss together.)

1. What do these verses show us about God's plan for Jesus?
2. Why do you think God waited for the "set time" to send His Son?
3. How can we show trust while waiting for God to answer our prayers?

FAMILY FAITH IN ACTION

Option 1: "The Waiting Game" (Interactive Experience)

1. Each family member shares one thing they're waiting for, big or small.
2. Set a timer for one minute and sit together in quiet stillness.
3. When the timer ends, talk about what it felt like to wait and what thoughts came to mind.

Connection:
Even when life feels quiet, God is always working behind the scenes. Waiting isn't wasted when our hearts stay open to His plan.

Option 2: "Promise Chain" (Creative Craft)

Supplies: Colored paper (any kind, construction or printer paper works), pens, tape, scissors, markers or pens, and a tape or glue stick.

1. Cut several strips of colored paper.
2. On each strip, write one of God's promises (examples: God is faithful, God provides, God keeps His word).
3. Loop and tape them together into a chain.
4. Hang it near your Advent area to remind your family that every promise is connected, and God's timing links them all together.

Connection:
God's promises are never broken. Each link reminds us that His plan is unfolding one piece at a time, just like it did when Jesus was born.

PERSONAL REFLECTION

Before you pray, take a moment to write or draw:
Write one sentence about something you're waiting for and how you want to trust God with it. (Example: "I'm waiting for something new, but I know God is preparing the right time for it.")

(Encourage each family member to write or share aloud if they'd like.)

FAMILY PRAYER TIME

Choose one person to lead the prayer tonight.
It can be as simple as thanking God for His perfect plan and the way every detail fits together in His timing. Ask Him to give your family patience, peace, and faith while you wait for the promises He's preparing to unfold.

THE CANDY CANE ☆

> The candy cane's shape looks like a shepherd's staff; Jesus, our Good Shepherd.

> The red stripes remind us of His love and sacrifice.

> Candy canes are often shared, just like God's love is meant to be shared with others.

> The white stands for forgiveness and a clean heart.

EVERY STRIPE TELLS A STORY, EVERY CURVE REMINDS US OF LOVE: JESUS IS OUR GOOD SHEPHERD.

DAY 14 ☆ THE CANDY CANE   JOHN 10:11

"I am the good shepherd. The good shepherd lays down His life for the sheep."
— John 10:11 (NIV)

BEFORE YOU BEGIN

Color in Day 14 on your Advent Tracker. Grab a candy cane if you have one, or imagine holding one in your hand. Today, we'll learn how this simple treat tells the story of Jesus, His love, His sacrifice, and His care for us as our Shepherd.

THE READING - THE STORY BEHIND THE CANE

The candy cane's shape, color, and sweetness each tell us something about Jesus. When turned upside down, it forms a J, for Jesus. When turned upright, it becomes a shepherd's staff, reminding us that Jesus is our Good Shepherd who guides and protects us.

The red stripes remind us of Jesus' sacrifice on the cross, and the white stands for His purity and forgiveness. Every time we see a candy cane, we can remember the sweet story of His love.

Read John 10:11 together. Talk about what it means that Jesus is the "Good Shepherd."

FAMILY READ-ALOUD SUMMARY

The candy cane tells the story of Jesus in a special way. It reminds us that He loves us, protects us, and gave His life for us. Whenever you see one, think of His love that never ends, sweet and strong.

STUDY & REFLECTION ON JOHN 10:11

All suggestions are optional; the most important thing is interacting with God's Word and connecting with what He wants to show you today.

1. **Read the passage slowly** — John 10:11.

2. **Write or draw a candy cane in your Bible margin or journal.** Inside the stripes, write or draw what makes Jesus a "Good Shepherd" to you.

3. **Make the connection** - Ask yourself: "How does Jesus guide me when I feel lost?" Write, draw, or talk about your answer together.

KEY THEMES

- Jesus is our Good Shepherd.
- His love is both protective and sacrificial.
- We can share His story in simple, joyful ways.

PRACTICAL APPLICATION

Today's kindness challenge, *give a candy cane or treat to someone as a reminder of God's love*, is a fun and meaningful way to share your faith.

- You can add a tag that says:

"THIS CANDY CANE IS SHAPED LIKE A SHEPHERD'S STAFF, A REMINDER THAT JESUS LOVES YOU!"

TEACHING POINTS

1. The shepherd's staff guides and protects the sheep, just like Jesus guides and protects us.
2. The stripes on the candy cane remind us of His sacrifice, and the sweetness reminds us that His love brings joy.
3. Even small things can carry big meaning when we see them through the eyes of faith.

SCRIPTURE CONNECTION

"The Lord is my shepherd; I lack nothing. He makes me lie down in green pastures, He leads me beside quiet waters, He refreshes my soul." — Psalm 23:1-3 (NIV)

FAMILY STUDY QUESTIONS

(Choose one or two to discuss together.)

1. What does a shepherd do for his sheep?
2. How is Jesus like a shepherd to us?
3. What can we learn from the candy cane about God's love?

FAMILY FAITH IN ACTION

Option 1: "Candy Cane Blessings" (Creative Action)

Supplies: Candy canes, ribbon or string, small note tags.

1. Write short messages like:
   - "Jesus loves you!" or "You are never alone."
2. Attach them to candy canes and give them to neighbors, friends, or teachers.

Connection:
Each candy cane becomes a sweet reminder of the love that Jesus freely gives.

Option 2: "Shepherd's Kindness Trail" (Action Game)

Supplies: Candy canes or small paper candy canes.

1. Hide candy canes or small paper ones around the house.
2. Each time someone finds one, they have to say one kind thing to another family member before they can keep it.

Connection:
It's a fun way to practice kindness, just like Jesus, our Good Shepherd, teaches us to love one another.

PERSONAL REFLECTION

Before you pray, take a moment to write or draw:
Write or draw one way you can follow Jesus' guidance this week. Example: "By being kind when I feel frustrated" or "By listening when someone needs a friend.")

(Encourage each family member to write or share aloud if they'd like.)

FAMILY PRAYER TIME

Choose one person to lead the prayer tonight.
It can be as simple as thanking Jesus for being our Shepherd and asking Him to help your family follow His love and share it with others.

DAY 15 GIFTS FIT FOR A KING MATTHEW 2:9-11

"On coming to the house, they saw the child with His mother Mary, and they bowed down and worshiped Him. Then they opened their treasures and presented Him with gifts of gold, frankincense, and myrrh." — Matthew 2:11 (NIV)

BEFORE YOU BEGIN

Color in Day 15 on your Advent Tracker. Find something shiny or beautiful nearby, a light, a star ornament, or even a wrapped gift. Take a moment to look at it and remember: the first Christmas gifts weren't toys or treats, they were treasures given to honor Jesus.

THE READING - WORSHIP IN GIVING

When the wise men finally found Jesus, they were filled with joy. They knelt down and worshiped Him, offering their most precious gifts, gold, frankincense, and myrrh. Each gift had meaning:
- Gold for a King.
- Frankincense for God's presence and worship.
- Myrrh for sacrifice and love.

Their gifts showed that Jesus wasn't just a baby; He was the promised Savior, worthy of all honor.

Read Matthew 2:9-11 together. Talk about what it means to give your best to Jesus, not just things, but love, time, and kindness.

FAMILY READ-ALOUD SUMMARY

The wise men gave their best to Jesus, gifts that showed love and worship. They remind us that giving isn't about what we have, but about offering our hearts.

STUDY & REFLECTION ON MATTHEW 2:9-11

All suggestions are optional; the most important thing is interacting with God's Word and connecting with what He wants to show you today.

1. **Read the passage slowly** — Matthew 2:9-11.

2. **Write or draw three "gifts" you can offer Jesus this week, like patience, kindness, or prayer in your Bible margin or journal.**
(Example: "I can give Jesus my time when I talk to Him in prayer.")

3. **Make the connection** - Ask yourself: "What does it mean to give my best to God?" Write, draw, or talk about your answer together.

KEY THEMES

- Giving is an act of worship.
- Every gift we give can honor Jesus.
- Our hearts are the greatest gift of all.

TEACHING POINTS

1. The wise men didn't bring what was easy; they brought what was meaningful.
2. Their gifts told the story of who Jesus was and who He would become.
3. When we give, we can worship too, through love, service, and gratitude.
4. Every time we give something with joy, we echo the gifts brought to the manger.

PRACTICAL APPLICATION

Today's kindness challenge, give a small act of service as your gift to Jesus, can be simple:

- Help someone without being asked, pray for a friend, or share a kind word.

EACH SMALL ACT OF SERVICE IS A WAY OF SAYING, "I GIVE THIS TO YOU, JESUS."

SCRIPTURE CONNECTION

"Each of you should give what you have decided in your heart to give, not reluctantly or under compulsion, for God loves a cheerful giver."
— 2 Corinthians 9:7 (NIV)

FAMILY STUDY QUESTIONS

(Choose one or two to discuss together.)

1. Why do you think the wise men brought those specific gifts?
2. What does giving mean to you?
3. How can our family give our best to God this week?

FAMILY FAITH IN ACTION

Option 1: "Gift to Jesus" (Creative Action)

Supplies: Paper, scissors, pens, and a small box or envelope.

1. Each person writes down one gift they want to give Jesus this week, a kind act, time in prayer, or a word of gratitude, and places it in the box.
2. Set the box under your Christmas tree as a reminder that Christmas is about giving to Him first.

Connection:
The wise men brought treasures for Jesus. Your gifts of love and faith are just as precious.

Option 2: "Serve Like the Wise Men" (Action Challenge)

1. Each family member chooses one person to serve quietly this week, without telling them in advance.
2. At the end of the week, share what you did and how it made you feel.

Connection:
The wise men gave from the heart. When you serve others in love, you're giving your best to Jesus too.

PERSONAL REFLECTION

Before you pray, take a moment to write or draw:
Write or draw one way you can give your best to God this week, not as a rule, but as worship. (Example: "By helping without being asked," or "By praying before I start my day.")

(Encourage each family member to write or share aloud if they'd like.)

FAMILY PRAYER TIME

Choose one person to lead the prayer tonight.
It can be as simple as thanking God for the joy of giving and asking Him to help your family give with hearts full of love, like the wise men.

DAY 16   A WARNING IN THE NIGHT   MATTHEW 2:12-13

"When they had gone, an angel of the Lord appeared to Joseph in a dream. 'Get up,' he said, 'take the child and His mother and escape to Egypt.'" — Matthew 2:13 (NIV)

BEFORE YOU BEGIN

Color in Day 16 on your Advent Tracker. If it's evening, dim the lights or light a candle. Close your eyes for a few seconds and imagine being fast asleep when suddenly you hear God's voice whisper in your heart: *"Get up. Go. I'll keep you safe."*

THE READING - GOD'S VOICE IN THE QUIET

After the wise men visited Jesus, an angel came to Joseph in a dream. The angel warned him that King Herod wanted to harm the child and told him to take Mary and Jesus to Egypt for safety. Even though it was the middle of the night, Joseph didn't wait. He obeyed right away, trusting that God knew what was best.

Read Matthew 2:12-13 together. Talk about how God sometimes guides us through gentle whispers, ideas, or nudges in our hearts.

FAMILY READ-ALOUD SUMMARY

Joseph listened to God, even when it meant leaving in the middle of the night. God's warning protected Jesus, and Joseph's obedience showed deep faith. When we listen and trust God, He leads us to safety and peace.

STUDY & REFLECTION ON MATTHEW 2:12-13

All suggestions are optional; the most important thing is interacting with God's Word and connecting with what He wants to show you today.

1. **Read the passage slowly** — Matthew 2:12-13.

2. **Write or draw what it means to "trust God's direction" in your Bible margin or journal.** (Example: "God, help me listen when You speak to my heart.")

3. **Make the connection** - Ask yourself: "How do I know when God is guiding me?" Write, draw, or talk about your answer together.

KEY THEMES

- God guides and protects His people.
- Obedience shows trust.
- Listening to God brings peace and safety.

PRACTICAL APPLICATION

Praying for someone who needs protection, peace, or courage is a simple way to listen and act like Joseph.

- You can even write their name in your bible or whisper their name during prayer tonight.

GOD DOESN'T JUST SPEAK IN BIG MOMENTS. HE GUIDES US EVERY DAY.

SCRIPTURE CONNECTION

"I will instruct you and teach you in the way you should go; I will counsel you with My loving eye on you." — Psalm 32:8 (NIV)

TEACHING POINTS

1. Joseph didn't argue or delay; he trusted God's direction immediately.
2. Sometimes, God's guidance comes when we least expect it, during quiet moments, dreams, or through His Word.
3. When we obey, even when we don't understand everything, we show that we believe He knows best.

FAMILY STUDY QUESTIONS

(Choose one or two to discuss together.)

1. How did God guide Joseph in this story?
2. Why is it important to listen to God, even when we're afraid?
3. How can our family practice listening for God together?

FAMILY FAITH IN ACTION

Option 1: "Prayer Lanterns" (Creative Action)

Supplies: Paper, markers, scissors, and tape.

1. Cut out paper lantern shapes and write the names of people you want God to protect or guide.
2. Hang them in a window or around your tree.

Connection:
Each lantern represents a prayer, a light shining in the dark, just like God's guidance in the night.

Option 2: Whisper Walk (or Sit & Listen)

1. Take a short family walk together, outside if you can, or even around your home. If walking isn't possible, simply sit together on your porch, balcony, or near a window.
2. Stay quiet for a minute or two and notice the sounds around you, the wind, birds, laughter, or even silence.
3. Afterward, share one small thing you noticed that reminded you of God's care or creation.

Connection:
Joseph listened in the quiet of the night, and so can we. When we pause and listen, we learn that God's voice can be heard not just in big moments, but in small, peaceful ones too.

PERSONAL REFLECTION

Before you pray, take a moment to write or draw:
Write or draw one way you can listen for God this week, maybe in prayer, during a quiet moment, or by reading His Word. (Example: "I'll listen by being still before bed and thanking God for the day.")

(Encourage each family member to write or share aloud if they'd like.)

FAMILY PRAYER TIME

Choose one person to lead the prayer tonight.
It can be as simple as thanking God for His protection and asking Him to help your family listen for His voice with faith and peace.

DAY 17   THE FAMILY FLEES TO EGYPT   MATTHEW 2:14-15

"So he got up, took the child and His mother during the night and left for Egypt, where he stayed until the death of Herod." — Matthew 2:14-15 (NIV)

BEFORE YOU BEGIN

Color in Day 17 on your Advent Tracker. Find a blanket and wrap it around your shoulders for a moment. Imagine how Mary and Joseph must have felt, leaving home in the dark, trusting God to keep them safe on the road ahead.

THE READING - TRUST ON THE JOURNEY

After Joseph's dream, he didn't hesitate. He woke up, gathered Mary and baby Jesus, and began the long journey to Egypt. It wasn't easy; they were tired, far from home, and unsure what would come next. But through every step, God was with them, guiding their path and protecting His Son.

Read Matthew 2:14-15 together. Talk about how God can protect and guide your family, too, even when life feels uncertain.

FAMILY READ-ALOUD SUMMARY

Joseph obeyed right away, and God led their family to safety in Egypt. Even when they were far from home, God never left them. He always keeps His promises and watches over His children.

STUDY & REFLECTION ON MATTHEW 2:14-15

All suggestions are optional; the most important thing is interacting with God's Word and connecting with what He wants to show you today.

1. **Read the passage slowly** — Matthew 2:14-15.

2. **Write or draw a path or road in your Bible margin or journal.** On the road, write words or draw pictures that show where you've seen God's protection or care.

3. **Make the connection** - Ask yourself: "When have I felt safe because of God's help?" Write, draw, or talk about your answer together.

KEY THEMES

- God's protection never fails.
- Trust means obeying even when the way is unclear.
- Faith grows stronger when we follow God's lead.

PRACTICAL APPLICATION

Being gentle with someone who seems upset or afraid is one way to show God's care.

TEACHING POINTS

1. Mary and Joseph didn't know what the road ahead would hold, but they trusted that God did.
2. Their faith reminds us that obedience isn't always easy, but God's direction always leads to safety and purpose.
3. Sometimes, God asks us to take brave steps, and His protection travels with us wherever we go.

SOMETIMES YOUR CALM WORDS OR SOFT TONE CAN REMIND OTHERS THAT THEY'RE NOT ALONE.

SCRIPTURE CONNECTION

"The Lord will keep you from all harm — He will watch over your life; the Lord will watch over your coming and going both now and forevermore."
— Psalm 121:7-8 (NIV)

FAMILY STUDY QUESTIONS

(Choose one or two to discuss together.)

1. How do you think Mary and Joseph felt leaving home at night?
2. What do you think helped them trust God during their journey?
3. How can we show trust in God as a family this week?

FAMILY FAITH IN ACTION

Option 1: "The Road of Trust" (Creative Action)

Supplies: Paper, crayons, or chalk.

1. Draw a winding path and label the turns with "faith," "courage," "love," and "obedience."
2. Each family member adds their name somewhere along the path to show that you're walking with God together.

Connection:
Even when the road is uncertain, God leads us step by step, and His light never fades.

Option 2: "Safe in His Hands" (Action Reflection)

1. Have each person hold a small object (a pebble, ornament, or heart cutout).
2. Say a short prayer: "God, thank You for holding me safe in Your hands."
3. Place all the objects in a bowl or jar labeled "God Protects Us."

Connection:
Just as God protected Jesus' family, He holds your family safely, too.

Closing Prayer

PERSONAL REFLECTION

Before you pray, take a moment to write or draw:
Write or draw one way you can show trust this week, maybe by praying before worrying, or being brave about something new.

(Encourage each family member to write or share aloud if they'd like.)

FAMILY PRAYER TIME

Choose one person to lead the prayer tonight.
It can be as simple as thanking God for His protection and asking Him to help your family trust His guidance through every season.

THE WREATH

The circle of the wreath reminds us of God's unending love.

The evergreen leaves represent everlasting life.

The candles remind us of the light of Christ.

The bow shows how love ties everything together.

GOD'S LOVE NEVER ENDS, IT CIRCLES AROUND US FOREVER.

DAY 18 — THE WREATH — ISAIAH 9:6

"For to us a child is born, to us a son is given, and the government will be on His shoulders. And He will be called Wonderful Counselor, Mighty God, Everlasting Father, Prince of Peace." — Isaiah 9:6 (NIV)

BEFORE YOU BEGIN

Color in Day 18 on your Advent Tracker. Look at your family's wreath, on a door, a table, or even drawn on paper. Notice it's a circle shape. It doesn't have a beginning or an end, just like God's love for us.

THE READING - A CIRCLE OF LOVE

The Christmas wreath is a circle to remind us of something eternal; God's love has no end. It's made with evergreens, which stay alive all year long, symbolizing everlasting life. Some wreaths have candles, each representing hope, peace, joy, and love, the gifts Jesus brings into our hearts.

When we hang a wreath, it's like saying, "God's love lives here."

Read Isaiah 9:6 together and talk about which name for Jesus stands out most to you today, Wonderful Counselor, Mighty God, Everlasting Father, or Prince of Peace.

FAMILY READ-ALOUD SUMMARY

The wreath reminds us that God's love never ends. Jesus came to bring peace, joy, hope, and love that last forever. Every time you see a wreath, remember that His presence is all around you.

STUDY & REFLECTION ON ISAIAH 9:6

All suggestions are optional; the most important thing is interacting with God's Word and connecting with what He wants to show you today.

1. **Read the passage slowly** — Isaiah 9:6.

2. **Write or draw a wreath in your Bible margin or journal.** Inside the circle, write one of the names of Jesus that means the most to you.

3. **Make the connection** - Ask yourself: "What does peace mean to me right now?" Write, draw, or talk about your answer together.

KEY THEMES

- God's love is eternal.
- Jesus brings peace and unity to every heart that welcomes Him.
- The wreath reminds us to keep Christ at the center of our home.

PRACTICAL APPLICATION

Bring peace wherever you go, through your words, smiles, or small acts of kindness.

TEACHING POINTS

1. A wreath is a circle shape, reminding us that God's love has no beginning or end. It always keeps going.
2. The greenery reminds us of life that never fades.
3. When we focus on Jesus, our homes and hearts can stay full of peace, even when the world feels busy or broken.

EVERY PEACEFUL MOMENT YOU CREATE BECOMES PART OF GOD'S CIRCLE OF LOVE.

SCRIPTURE CONNECTION

"Peace I leave with you; My peace I give you. I do not give to you as the world gives. Do not let your hearts be troubled and do not be afraid." — John 14:27 (NIV)

FAMILY STUDY QUESTIONS

(Choose one or two to discuss together.)

1. What does the circular shape of a wreath remind you of?
2. Which name for Jesus means the most to you today, and why?
3. How can our family share peace this week?

FAMILY FAITH IN ACTION

Option 1: "The Ripple of Peace" (Interactive Family Experiment)

Supplies: A bowl of water and small pebbles (or buttons).

1. Each person takes a turn, gently dropping a pebble into the water and watching the ripples spread.
2. As you watch, say one kind word or peaceful phrase ("I forgive," "I love you," "I'm thankful for you").

Connection:
Peace spreads like ripples; one small act or word can move outward and touch many lives. Just as a wreath's circle keeps going, peace keeps moving when we share it.

Option 2: "Movie Moment of Peace" (Family Reflection Night)

1. Pick a favorite Christmas movie to watch together, something with a theme of love, hope, or forgiveness (The Star, The Grinch, or A Charlie Brown Christmas works wonderfully).
2. Before pressing play, pray together:
   "God, help us see Your peace in this story tonight."
3. After the movie, take a minute to talk:
   - Where did you see someone showing peace or love?
   - Which character reminded you most of Jesus' peace?

Connection:
Just like the wreath reminds us that God's love has no end, these stories remind us that peace and kindness always come full circle, just like God's love in our lives.

PERSONAL REFLECTION

Before you pray, take a moment to write or draw:
Write or draw one place in your life where you want God's peace to grow, at school, at work, or in your home.

(Encourage each family member to write or share aloud if they'd like.)

FAMILY PRAYER TIME

Choose one person to lead the prayer tonight.
It can be as simple as thanking Jesus for being our peace and asking Him to help your family be a circle of love to others.

DAY 19   RETURN TO NAZARETH   MATTHEW 2:19-23

"After Herod died, an angel of the Lord appeared in a dream to Joseph in Egypt and said, 'Get up, take the child and His mother and go to the land of Israel, for those who were trying to take the child's life are dead.'" — Matthew 2:19-20 (NIV)

BEFORE YOU BEGIN

Color in Day 19 on your Advent Tracker. Look around your home for a moment, at your family, your cozy spaces, your lights, or decorations. Just like Joseph and Mary, we can thank God for the safety, peace, and love we find in our homes.

THE READING - HOME AGAIN

After Herod died, God told Joseph it was time to return home. The journey to Nazareth was long, but now the family could rest and live in peace. They had trusted God through fear, travel, and change, and now they were safe again under His care.

Jesus would grow up in Nazareth, surrounded by love and the everyday beauty of ordinary life. It's a reminder that God is present not only in miracles but in the simple moments of home.

Read Matthew 2:19-23 together. Talk about how it feels to come home after a long trip, and how God gives peace to those who trust Him.

FAMILY READ-ALOUD SUMMARY

After so many journeys, the family finally returned home. They had seen God's protection, guidance, and love in every step. Now, their hearts were full of gratitude. Home was no longer just a place; it was the space where God's peace lived with them.

STUDY & REFLECTION ON MATTHEW 2:19-23

All suggestions are optional; the most important thing is interacting with God's Word and connecting with what He wants to show you today.

KEY THEMES

- God keeps His promises of safety and peace.
- Home is sacred when filled with love.
- Obedience and trust lead us back to peace.

1. **Read the passage slowly** — Matthew 2:19-23.

2. **Write or draw something that represents "home" to you; it could be a person, a memory, or a favorite place in your Bible margin or journal.**

3. **Make the connection** - Ask yourself: "What makes a place feel peaceful?" Write, draw, or talk about your answer together.

TEACHING POINTS

1. Joseph's faith didn't stop once the danger was over. He still listened, obeyed, and trusted God's next instructions.
2. Returning home wasn't just a physical journey; it was a spiritual one, too.
3. God's protection continues long after the storm ends.

FAMILY STUDY QUESTIONS

(Choose one or two to discuss together.)

1. Why do you think God called the family back to Nazareth?
2. How do you think they felt being home again?
3. What can we do to make our home a place of peace and love?

PRACTICAL APPLICATION

Do something that makes home feel more loving, which can be as simple as helping with dinner, cleaning a room, or making someone laugh.

WHEN WE CARE FOR OUR HOME, WE BUILD A SPACE WHERE GOD'S PEACE CAN LIVE.

SCRIPTURE CONNECTION

"And over all these virtues put on love, which binds them all together in perfect unity. Let the peace of Christ rule in your hearts, since as members of one body you were called to peace."
— Colossians 3:14–15 (NIV)

FAMILY FAITH IN ACTION

Option 1: "Home Blessing Walk" (Interactive Family Activity)

1. Walk through your home together and pause in a few rooms, the kitchen, bedrooms, or living area.
2. In each spot, say a short prayer of blessing (like "God, thank You for laughter here," or "God, bring peace to this room").
3. If you like, place a small paper heart in each room to remind you that this home belongs to God.

Connection:
Just like the Holy Family returned home safely, we can fill our homes with God's peace and presence every day.

Option 2: "The Taste of Home" (Creative Action)

Supplies: Ingredients for your favorite family snack or meal.

1. Cook or bake together and share stories about your favorite memories of home.
2. Before you eat, pray together and thank God for the blessings that make your home special.

Connection:
Home is more than a place; it's the love, laughter, and peace that God brings when we gather together.

PERSONAL REFLECTION

Before you pray, take a moment to write or draw:
Write or draw one way you can make your home feel more peaceful this week.
(Example: "I'll use kind words," or "I'll help keep our home tidy.")

(Encourage each family member to write or share aloud if they'd like.)

FAMILY PRAYER TIME

Choose one person to lead the prayer tonight.
It can be as simple as thanking God for your home and asking Him to fill every room with His peace and love.

ANGELS FROM THE REALMS OF GLORY

DAY 20 SIMEON AND ANNA REJOICE LUKE 2:25-38

"Simeon took Him in his arms and praised God, saying: 'Sovereign Lord, as You have promised, You may now dismiss Your servant in peace. For my eyes have seen Your salvation.'" — Luke 2:28-30 (NIV)

BEFORE YOU BEGIN

Color in Day 20 on your Advent Tracker. Close your eyes and take a deep breath. Think of something you've waited for, and how it felt when the waiting was finally over. That's what Simeon and Anna felt the first time they saw baby Jesus.

THE READING - WAITING, WATCHING, REJOICING

Simeon and Anna were two faithful people who spent their days praying in the temple. They trusted that one day they would see God's promise, the Savior. When Mary and Joseph brought Jesus to the temple, Simeon's heart overflowed with joy. He held the baby and praised God, saying that his eyes had seen salvation. Anna, a prophetess, also praised God and told everyone about the child who would bring redemption.

Both had waited a lifetime, and in that moment, their joy was complete.

Read Luke 2:25-38 together and talk about how it feels when something long-awaited finally happens.

FAMILY READ-ALOUD SUMMARY

Simeon and Anna waited and prayed for many years, trusting God's promise. When they finally saw Jesus, their hearts were full of joy and peace. Their story reminds us that waiting on God is never wasted; His timing is always perfect.

STUDY & REFLECTION ON LUKE 2:25-38

All suggestions are optional; the most important thing is interacting with God's Word and connecting with what He wants to show you today.

1. **Read the passage slowly** — Luke 2:25-38.

2. **Write or draw something you're waiting or praying for in your Bible margin or journal.**

3. **Make the connection** - Ask yourself: "What helps me trust God when I have to wait?" Write, draw, or talk about your answer together.

KEY THEMES

- God always keeps His promises.
- Waiting builds faith and trust.
- Joy comes when we see God's plan unfold.

PRACTICAL APPLICATION

Doing something thoughtful for an older neighbor or family member is a wonderful way to honor those who've waited, prayed, and led by faith.

CALL, WRITE, OR SPEND TIME WITH SOMEONE WHO'S TAUGHT YOU ABOUT PATIENCE OR KINDNESS.

TEACHING POINTS

1. Simeon and Anna remind us that faith sometimes means waiting and trusting even when we can't see what's coming.
2. Their patience became praise when they finally saw God's promise.
3. God's timing may not be fast, but it's always perfect and filled with purpose.

SCRIPTURE CONNECTION

"Let us not become weary in doing good, for at the proper time we will reap a harvest if we do not give up."
— Galatians 6:9 (NIV)

FAMILY STUDY QUESTIONS

(Choose one or two to discuss together.)

1. How do you think Simeon and Anna felt when they saw Jesus?
2. Why is waiting sometimes hard, but worth it?
3. What can our family do to wait well and trust God together?

FAMILY FAITH IN ACTION

Option 1: "Joy Journal" (Creative Family Activity)

Supplies: Paper, crayons, or a notebook.

1. Have each family member make a "Joy Page."
2. Write or draw three things that bring joy, and one thing you're still waiting for but want to trust God with.
3. Place the pages in a visible spot as a reminder to praise while you wait.

Connection:
Simeon and Anna found joy after years of waiting. Joy grows when we remember what God has already done.

Option 2: "Joyful Moments Movie Night" (Family Reflection)

1. Choose a movie that shows patience, kindness, or faith (The Nativity Story or The Polar Express).
2. Before pressing play, pray together:
   "God, help us see joy in every part of Your story."
3. Afterward, share one scene that reminded you of hope or faithfulness.

Connection:
Even in stories and movies, we see pieces of God's message, joy after waiting, light after darkness, peace after uncertainty.

PERSONAL REFLECTION

Before you pray, take a moment to write or draw:
Write or draw one word that reminds you of joy and decorate it! (Example: "Hope," "Light," "Faith," or "Peace.")

(Encourage each family member to write or share aloud if they'd like.)

FAMILY PRAYER TIME

Choose one person to lead the prayer tonight.
It can be as simple as thanking God for the joy of His promises and asking Him to help your family trust His timing.

Just as the bells announce celebration, our voices and actions can proclaim the name of Jesus, the One who brings light and life to all.

DAY 21 — THE NAME ABOVE ALL NAMES — PHILIPPIANS 2:9-11

"At the name of Jesus every knee should bow." — Philippians 2:10 (NIV)

BEFORE YOU BEGIN

Color in Day 21 on your Advent Tracker. Take a quiet moment to whisper Jesus' name and think about what it means to you. Names have power, and His name is the one that brings peace, hope, and life to all who call on Him.

THE READING - EVERY KNEE WILL BOW

After His obedience and humility, Jesus was lifted higher than anyone else. God gave Him a name above every other name, so that at the name of Jesus, every knee will bow and every tongue confess that He is Lord.

It's a reminder that the tiny baby in the manger was and is the King of Kings. His name carries authority, love, and salvation for all who believe.

Read Philippians 2:9-11 together and thank God for the gift of Jesus' name.

FAMILY READ-ALOUD SUMMARY

The name of Jesus is powerful because it shows who He is, the Savior and King of the world. When we speak His name with love and faith, we remember that He is with us every moment, bringing light into darkness and peace into our hearts.

STUDY & REFLECTION ON PHILIPPIANS 2:9-11

All suggestions are optional; the most important thing is interacting with God's Word and connecting with what He wants to show you today.

KEY THEMES

- The power of Jesus' name.
- Worship and reverence for Christ.
- Humility leads to honor.

1. **Read the passage slowly** — Philippians 2:9-11.

2. **Write or draw the word "Jesus" in large, decorative letters in your Bible margin or journal.** Around it, write words or draw symbols that describe who He is to you. For example, Friend, Savior, Light, Hope, King.

3. **Make the connection** - Ask yourself: "What does it mean to call Jesus 'Lord' today, in my home, school, or heart?" Write, draw, or talk about your answer together.

PRACTICAL APPLICATION

Every word of encouragement rings like a bell, spreading faith farther than you know.

TEACHING POINTS

LET YOUR WORDS CARRY LIGHT AND LOVE INTO SOMEONE'S DAY.

1. Jesus' obedience and humility led to His exaltation, a reminder that God honors faithful hearts.
2. His name is more than a word; it's a promise of salvation and presence.
3. When we honor Jesus' name, we declare His lordship over our lives.

SCRIPTURE CONNECTION

"And I will do whatever you ask in my name, so that the Father may be glorified in the Son." — John 14:13 (NIV)

FAMILY STUDY QUESTIONS

(Choose one or two to discuss together.)

1. Why is the name of Jesus so special?
2. What does it mean to honor His name?
3. How can our family bring glory to His name today?

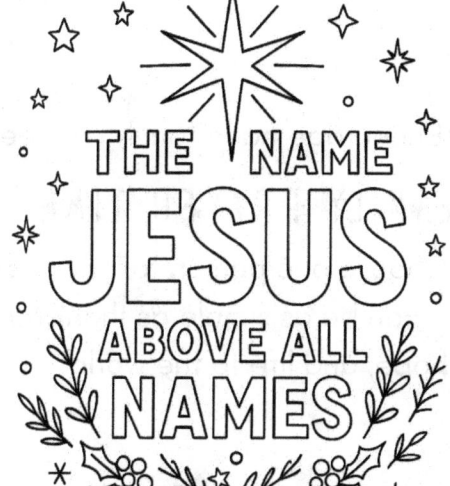

FAMILY FAITH IN ACTION

Option 1: "Name of Jesus Wall"
(Creative Display)

Supplies: Poster board or paper, markers or crayons, and optional tape.

1. Write or draw the name "Jesus" in the center of a poster board.
2. Around it, each family member adds words or phrases that describe what His name means to them.
3. Hang it somewhere you'll see it often as a reminder to speak His name with love.

Connection:
Each word you add is an act of worship. Together, your family is creating a picture of praise.

Option 2: "King of Kings Movie Night"
(Faith Through Film)

1. Gather as a family to watch the movie King of Kings, 2025 (or choose another Jesus film your family enjoys).
2. As you watch, notice how people speak His name, with awe, love, or faith, and let it stir worship in your own heart.
3. Afterward, talk about the moments that showed Jesus' strength, compassion, or humility.

Connection:
Every story about Jesus reminds us why His name is powerful.

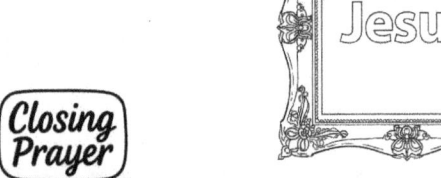

Closing Prayer

PERSONAL REFLECTION

Before you pray, take a moment to write or draw:
Write one sentence about what Jesus' name means to you today.

(Encourage each family member to write or share aloud if they'd like.)

FAMILY PRAYER TIME

Choose one person to lead the prayer tonight.
It can be as simple as thanking God for the name of Jesus, the name that brings peace, hope, and life to the world.

The red "petals" of a poinsettia are actually colorful leaves called bracts. The real flowers are the tiny yellow buds in the center! (Just like God, beauty often hides in the details.)

In Mexico, it's called "La Flor de Nochebuena," the Flower of the Holy Night.

The poinsettia's shape looks like the Star of Bethlehem, which led the wise men to Jesus. Its red leaves remind us of God's love, and the green symbolizes everlasting life.

DAY 22   THE POINSETTIA   2 CORINTHIANS 9:15

"Thanks be to God for His indescribable gift!" — 2 Corinthians 9:15 (NIV)

BEFORE YOU BEGIN

Color in Day 22 on your Advent Tracker. Take a moment to think about your favorite Christmas gifts, not the ones that cost the most, but the ones that made you feel most loved. The poinsettia reminds us that the best gifts come from the heart, not the store.

THE READING - A GIFT THAT BLOOMED

The story of the poinsettia comes from long ago, when a young girl in Mexico wanted to bring a gift to Jesus during a Christmas celebration. She had no money for fancy presents, so she gathered a handful of roadside weeds and placed them at the altar with a humble prayer. In that moment, the weeds burst into bright red blooms, a miracle of beauty born from a simple act of love.

The poinsettia became a symbol of heartfelt giving, the reminder that even small gifts, when offered with love, can glorify God.

Read 2 Corinthians 9:15 together and talk about why Jesus is called "the indescribable gift." What makes Him the greatest gift ever given?

FAMILY READ-ALOUD SUMMARY

God's love is the greatest gift the world has ever received. When we give to others, even in small, quiet ways, we reflect that same love. The poinsettia reminds us that when our hearts are filled with gratitude, our gifts bloom into something beautiful.

STUDY & REFLECTION ON 2 CORINTHIANS 9:15

All suggestions are optional; the most important thing is interacting with God's Word and connecting with what He wants to show you today.

1. **Read the passage slowly** — 2 Corinthians 9:15.

2. **Write or draw a poinsettia flower. Inside its petals, write the names of people you can bless with your time or creativity this week in your Bible margin or journal.**

3. **Make the connection** - Ask yourself: "What can I make or do that would show someone God's love?" Write, draw, or talk about your answer together.

KEY THEMES

- Giving is a way to show gratitude to God.
- The best gifts are handmade by the heart.
- Love transforms even the smallest offering.

PRACTICAL APPLICATION

Today is all about giving from the heart! Make or share something simple, a drawing, snack, or note, and tell the person, "God put you on my heart today."

IT'S A BEAUTIFUL WAY TO LET GOD'S LOVE FLOW THROUGH YOUR HANDS.

TEACHING POINTS

1. The bright red leaves of the poinsettia remind us of Jesus' love, pure, bold, and freely given.
2. Like the girl's weeds turned to flowers, God takes what we give in love and turns it into something wonderful.
3. When we give with open hearts, we reflect the love of the One who gave us everything.

SCRIPTURE CONNECTION

"Every good and perfect gift is from above, coming down from the Father of the heavenly lights." — James 1:17 (NIV)

FAMILY STUDY QUESTIONS

(Choose one or two to discuss together.)

1. Why do you think God values gifts from the heart more than expensive ones?
2. How do small acts of love reflect God's big love for us?
3. What kind of gift could you make or give this week that shows someone they're special?

FAMILY FAITH IN ACTION

Option 1: "Bloom of Blessings" (Creative Family Craft)

Supplies: Red and green paper, scissors, and tape.

1. Cut out large red petals and smaller green leaves.
2. On each petal, write one way your family can show love this week.
3. Arrange them into a big paper poinsettia and hang it as a reminder that love is what makes us bloom.

Connection:
When each person adds their "petal," your family's love becomes one beautiful gift to God.

Option 2: "Give What You Have" (Action-Based Family Challenge)

1. Each person finds one thing they already own, a toy, book, or item they love, and chooses to give it away this week to bless someone else.
2. Remember, what makes a gift special is the love behind it, not the size, cost, or how fancy it is.

Connection:
Like the girl in the poinsettia story, giving from what we already have reminds us that God treasures gifts given from the heart.

Closing Prayer

PERSONAL REFLECTION

Before you pray, take a moment to write or draw:
Write or draw one "gift from the heart" you want to give Jesus this Christmas, something only He sees.

(Encourage each family member to write or share aloud if they'd like.)

FAMILY PRAYER TIME

Choose one person to lead the prayer tonight.
It can be as simple as thanking God for His indescribable gift, Jesus, and asking Him to fill your hearts with joy in giving.

Come, they told me,
pa rum pum pum pum
A newborn King to see,
pa rum pum pum pum
Our finest gifts we bring,
pa rum pum pum pum...

DAY 23   THE GREATEST GIFT OF ALL   JOHN 3:16

"For God so loved the world that he gave his one and only Son, that whoever believes in him shall not perish but have eternal life." — John 3:16 (NIV)

BEFORE YOU BEGIN

Color in Day 23 on your Advent Tracker. Think about the gifts wrapped and waiting under your tree, and then think about the greatest gift of all, Jesus. His gift can't be bought, wrapped, or broken; it lasts forever.

THE READING - GOD'S GREATEST GIFT

On the first Christmas, God gave the world something no one else could. His Son! Jesus came to bring light, hope, and forgiveness to every heart. That's why we celebrate Christmas, not just because Jesus was born, but because His birth was the beginning of the greatest love story ever told.

Like the little drummer boy, we don't have to bring expensive gifts. What God wants most is our hearts, our worship, our kindness, and our love for others.

FAMILY READ-ALOUD SUMMARY

God gave us His Son because He loves us more than we can imagine. Every time we show love to others, we're giving a piece of that same gift back to the world. Even the smallest acts, a smile, a prayer, a helping hand, can reflect the heart of Jesus.

STUDY & REFLECTION ON JOHN 3:16

All suggestions are optional; the most important thing is interacting with God's Word and connecting with what He wants to show you today.

KEY THEMES

- God's greatest gift is love.
- True giving reflects the heart of God.
- We can share Jesus' love through simple acts of kindness.

 1. **Read the passage slowly** — John 3:16.

2. **Write or draw a heart or gift box. Inside, list three things God's love has given you: hope, forgiveness, peace, or courage in your Bible margin or journal.**

3. **Make the connection** - Ask yourself: "How does knowing I'm loved by God change the way I see myself and others?" Write, draw, or talk about your answer together.

PRACTICAL APPLICATION

Doing something kind in secret isn't just about giving; it's about reflecting God's kind of love.

TEACHING POINTS

1. God's love is the reason behind Christmas; it's what started it all.
2. Jesus came so that everyone could have hope and eternal life.
3. The best way to celebrate is by giving love away, just like God did.

HE LOVED US BEFORE WE EVER NOTICED, AND SOMETIMES THE QUIETEST GIFTS SAY THE MOST.

SCRIPTURE CONNECTION

"But God demonstrates his own love for us in this: While we were still sinners, Christ died for us." — Romans 5:8 (NIV)

FAMILY STUDY QUESTIONS

(Choose one or two to discuss together.)

1. How does it feel to know God loves you personally?
2. Why do you think God gave us Jesus instead of something else?
3. How can we remind each other of that love even after Christmas?

FAMILY FAITH IN ACTION

Option 1: "Unwrap the Gift" (Symbolic Family Moment)

Supplies: A small wrapped box (can be empty) or a wrapped cross, ornament, or heart.

1. Gather as a family and unwrap the box together while reading John 3:16.
2. Inside, place a small note that says, "Jesus, the Greatest Gift of All."

Connection:
This simple act reminds families that every gift we open points back to the one gift that changed everything, Jesus.

Option 2: "Letters to Jesus" (Gratitude Keepsake)

Supplies: Paper, pens, envelopes, and a small box or jar.

1. Each person writes a short letter to Jesus, thanking Him for His love or telling Him what they want to give Him this Christmas.
2. Fold and place the letters in the jar or under the tree.

Connection:
These letters are gifts from the heart, words of love offered back to the One who gave us everything.

Closing Prayer

PERSONAL REFLECTION

Before you pray, take a moment to write or draw:
Write or draw one "gift of love" you can offer Jesus this Christmas.

(Encourage each family member to write or share aloud if they'd like.)

FAMILY PRAYER TIME

Choose one person to lead the prayer tonight.
I can be as simple as thanking God for sending Jesus, the greatest gift of all, and asking Him to fill your family with a love that keeps on giving.

DAY 24   THE MANGER MOMENT   LUKE 2:6-7

"While they were there, the time came for the baby to be born, and she gave birth to her firstborn, a son. She wrapped him in cloths and placed him in a manger, because there was no guest room available for them." — Luke 2:6-7 (NIV)

BEFORE YOU BEGIN

Color in Day 24 on your Advent Tracker. Then turn off most of the lights and light one candle or soft lamp. Sit together quietly and imagine that manger scene, the air still, the stars glowing, and the sound of a baby's first cry. The world didn't know it yet, but everything had changed.

THE READING - THE MOMENT HEAVEN TOUCHED EARTH

It happened quietly. No trumpets, no crowds, no grand announcement, just the sound of new life. Mary wrapped her baby in soft cloth and laid Him in a manger meant for animals. The Savior of the world arrived in the humblest way possible.

This was God's plan to show that His love would reach everyone, from the highest to the lowest. Jesus' first bed was not a palace crib but a manger, reminding us that God meets us in the most unexpected places.

FAMILY READ-ALOUD SUMMARY

Jesus was born in a stable, surrounded by love, not luxury. God could have chosen anywhere for His Son to be born, but He chose a manger, showing us that His love is for everyone. That's what makes this night so holy.

STUDY & REFLECTION ON LUKE 2:6-7

All suggestions are optional; the most important thing is interacting with God's Word and connecting with what He wants to show you today.

1. **Read the passage slowly** — Luke 2:6-7.

2. **Write or draw a simple manger. Inside, write one word that describes what Jesus' birth means to you: Peace, Hope, Joy, Love, or Grace in your Bible margin or journal.**

3. **Make the connection** - Ask yourself: "Where do I see God in the quiet moments of my life?" Write, draw, or talk about your answer together.

KEY THEMES

- God's love shines brightest in humility.
- Jesus came quietly, but His presence changed everything.
- True peace begins in simple, surrendered hearts.

TEACHING POINTS

1. God's ways are different from ours. He often chooses the simple to show His greatness.
2. Jesus' birth in a manger reminds us that He understands every part of life, even hardship.
3. The manger was the first throne of the King of Kings.

PRACTICAL APPLICATION

Spend tonight in stillness. Listen to soft Christmas music, light a candle, or sit by your tree.

LET PEACE FILL YOUR HOME AS YOU PREPARE YOUR HEART FOR TOMORROW'S JOY.

SCRIPTURE CONNECTION

"Who, being in very nature God, did not consider equality with God something to be used to his own advantage; rather, he made himself nothing by taking the very nature of a servant, being made in human likeness." — Philippians 2:6-7 (NIV)

FAMILY STUDY QUESTIONS

(Choose one or two to discuss together.)

1. If you had been in Bethlehem that night, what would you have wanted to give baby Jesus?
2. What does the manger story teach us about what truly matters this Christmas?
3. How can we keep the joy and wonder of Jesus' birth in our hearts after Christmas morning?

FAMILY FAITH IN ACTION

Option 1: "Build the Manger" (Simple Family Craft)

Supplies: Sticks, paper strips, Legos, or popsicle sticks.

1. Work together to build a small manger.
2. Inside, place slips of paper where each person writes a prayer of thanks to Jesus.
3. Leave it near your nativity or under your tree tonight.

Connection:
Your manger holds something more special than straw, the gratitude and love your family gives back to Jesus tonight.

Option 2: "Christmas Eve Quiet Wonder" (Cozy Christmas Eve Pause)

1. Sit together in silence for one minute, imagining the animals settling into the stable for the night and the manger waiting quietly for its King.
2. Think about Mary and Joseph preparing for Jesus' arrival and how still the world must have felt the night before the Savior was born.
3. After a minute, invite everyone to share one simple word that captures what they hope to carry into Christmas morning. (Examples include peace, joy, hope, love, wonder.)
4. Close with a soft prayer or the first line of "O Holy Night."

Connection:
Every quiet moment tonight helps us remember the wonder of Christmas, that Jesus came close, and His peace still fills the world.

PERSONAL REFLECTION

Before you pray, take a moment to write or draw:
Write or draw what the manger means to you, God's humility, love, peace, or nearness.

(Encourage each family member to write or share aloud if they'd like.)

FAMILY PRAYER TIME

Choose one person to lead the prayer tonight.
It can be as simple as thanking God for sending His Son to the world in love and humility. Ask Him to fill your home with peace as you wait for the joy of Christmas morning.

DAY 25 — THE BIRTH OF JESUS — LUKE 2:8-20

"Glory to God in the highest heaven, and on earth peace to those on whom his favor rests." — Luke 2:14 (NIV)

BEFORE YOU BEGIN

This is it, Day 25! Color in the final day on your Advent Tracker and take a deep breath. Christmas has come. The waiting is over. Before the day begins, gather your family and read Luke 2:8-20 aloud, the story of the shepherds, the angels, and the joy that changed the world forever.

THE READING - THE BIRTH OF JESUS (LUKE 2:8-20, NIV)

And there were shepherds living out in the fields nearby, keeping watch over their flocks at night. An angel of the Lord appeared to them, and the glory of the Lord shone around them, and they were terrified. But the angel said to them, "Do not be afraid. I bring you good news that will cause great joy for all the people. Today in the town of David a Savior has been born to you; he is the Messiah, the Lord. This will be a sign to you: You will find a baby wrapped in cloths and lying in a manger."

Suddenly a great company of the heavenly host appeared with the angel, praising God and saying,

"Glory to God in the highest heaven, and on earth peace to those on whom his favor rests."

When the angels had left them and gone into heaven, the shepherds said to one another, "Let's go to Bethlehem and see this thing that has happened, which the Lord has told us about."

So they hurried off and found Mary and Joseph, and the baby, who was lying in the manger. When they had seen him, they spread the word concerning what had been told them about this child, and all who heard it were amazed at what the shepherds said to them. But Mary treasured up all these things and pondered them in her heart. The shepherds returned, glorifying and praising God for all the things they had heard and seen, which were just as they had been told.

FAMILY READ-ALOUD SUMMARY

Today, we join that same song of praise, because God's gift wasn't just for one night, but for every heart that believes. As your family celebrates, carry this truth: **the story of Christmas doesn't end in the manger, it begins there.**

REFLECT & REJOICE - THE GIFT THAT REMAINS

REFLECTION PROMPTS

(Choose one or two to discuss together.)

1. What have you learned or rediscovered about God's love during this Advent journey?
2. How has this season changed the way you see Jesus, and the way you live?
3. What gift will you carry from this Advent season into the new year: peace, joy, faith, gratitude, or love?

A CHRISTMAS PRAYER

"GOD, THANK YOU FOR THE GIFT OF JESUS, THE LIGHT OF THE WORLD AND THE HOPE OF OUR HEARTS. AS WE CELEBRATE TODAY, HELP US KEEP OUR EYES ON YOU.
FILL OUR HOME WITH PEACE, JOY, AND LOVE THAT LASTS LONG AFTER CHRISTMAS MORNING. AMEN."

FINAL THOUGHT FOR FAMILIES

As the wrapping paper is opened and laughter fills the room, remember, the greatest gift is already yours. Carry Jesus with you into every moment of this day and every day that follows.

EVENING FAMILY REFLECTION

When the house grows quiet and the lights begin to dim, take one last moment together. Sit by the tree, the manger, or wherever your family gathers. No reading, no activity, just gratitude.

Take turns sharing one thing you want to remember from this Advent journey. It could be a verse, a lesson, or something you felt God teach you.

After each person shares, turn off one light in the room until only the softest glow remains, a reminder that even when the day ends, **the Light of the World still shines.**

CHRISTMAS NOTES

Nativity Scene

```
W L B A B Y J E S U S E X E J R
I E V S D R E H P E H S E Y O M
S G I F T S C V Q U X V O D U E
E I Y T L M I Q C C G E L Z F E
M W R S T A B L E R C R Z Y V V
E D G C Z C Y X M A I A A X V C
N I J O B H H I E K E B N T M A
Z A L O L J J P M X Y P M G S M
D N O G S D H I V M R S Z D E E
M I V N O E R R A J A H R L F L
C M E B E A P N R J M S P D I D
V A C H C H G H G Y P Z O P M O
B L L L D E K X U J M N M R G J
S S E T R S W K A E K Z Z Z P P
L F A I T H M E H E L H T E B O
F W C G W H O L Y F A M I L Y Y
```

ANGEL	ANIMALS	BABY JESUS
BETHLEHEM	CAMEL	CRIB
DONKEY	FAITH	GIFTS
GOLD	HOLY FAMILY	JOSEPH
LOVE	MANGER	MARY
MIRACLE	MYRRH	PEACE
SHEPHERDS	STABLE	STAR
WISE MEN		

CONNECT THE DOTS TO COMPLETE THE PICTURE. NEXT, COLOR THE PICTURE

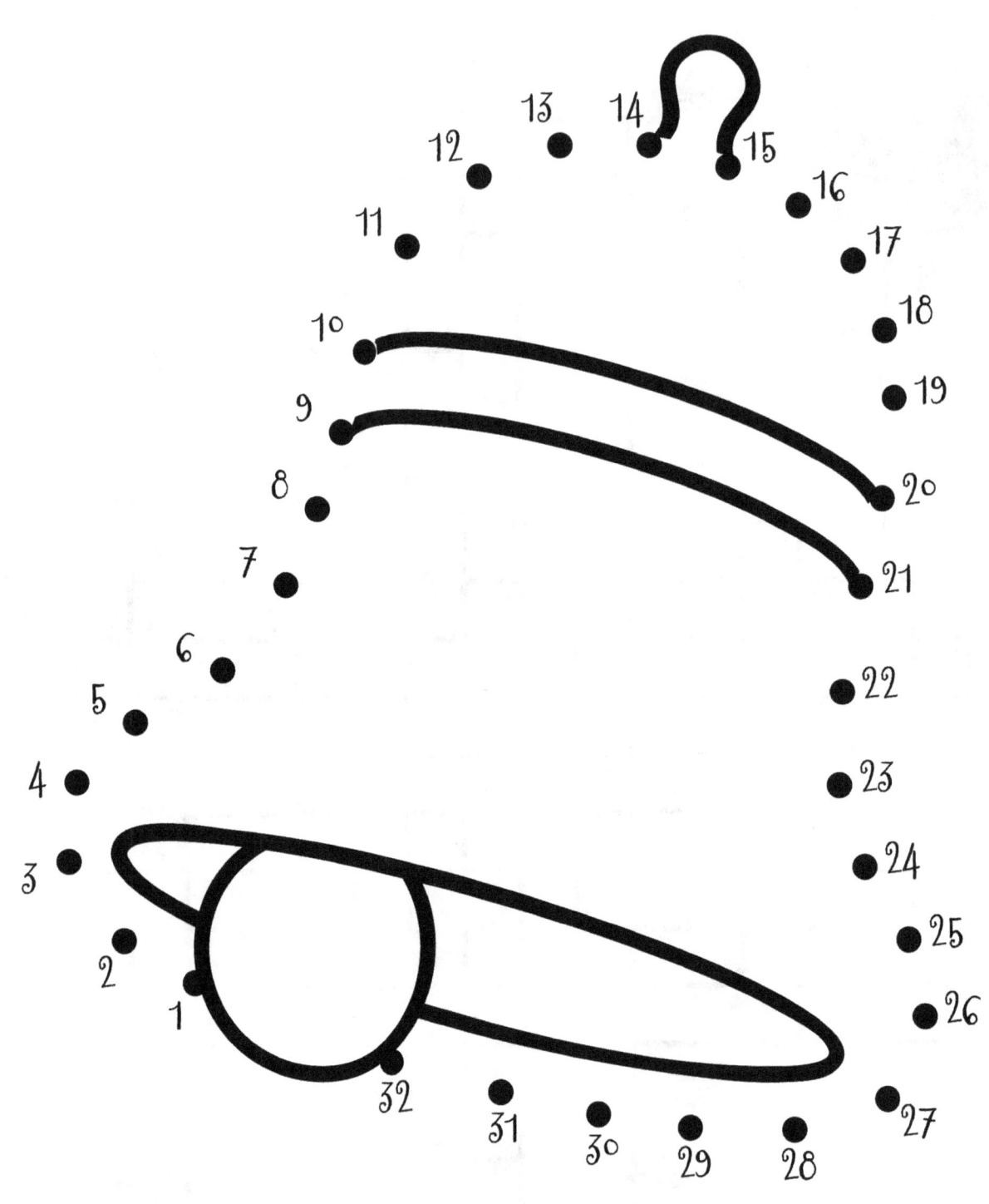

TIC - TAC - TOE

Christmas Trees

```
A A S N G U W K R E I N D E E R
Z L P O S A N T A A M P Q Z H J
W Y R I T Y J A H O K A H E O N
H T G T N U D N H G I E L S L R
L I D I E E Q G A R L A N D I G
X V S D M G C E N V G C S B D H
H I E A A Q Y L V R A T S X A A
E T N R N X W O N S T H G H Y H
V A A T R L J T S P A R K L E B
E N C E O J I O I J B N D F D A
R X Y B R B W G Y N S L L E B U
G K D U N W C H H B S Y S J Z B
R G N I K C O T S T O E O E Y L
E J A E V I T S E F S T L E U E
E I C U D R I B B O N S X K E S
N P R E S E N T S P M O B O L B
```

ANGEL	BAUBLES	BELLS
CANDY CANES	EVERGREEN	FESTIVE
GARLAND	HOLIDAY	JOY
LIGHTS	NATIVITY	ORNAMENTS
PINE	PRESENTS	REINDEER
RIBBONS	SANTA	SLEIGH
SNOW	SPARKLE	STAR
STOCKING	TINSEL	TRADITION
WREATH		

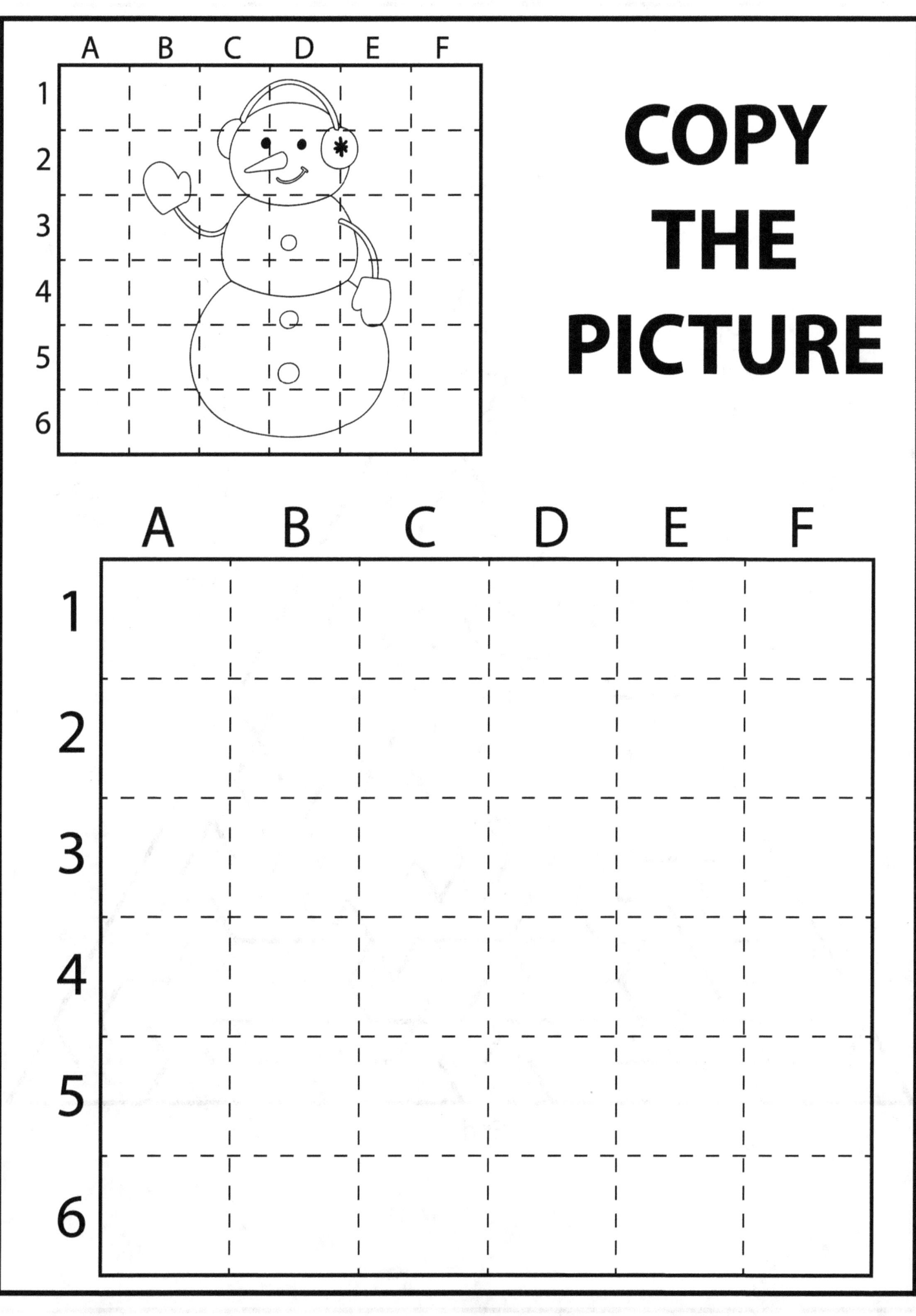

Maze

Start

End

www.ingramcontent.com/pod-product-compliance
Lightning Source LLC
Chambersburg PA
CBHW080415170426
43194CB00015B/2816